The Best of Roswell

The Best of Roswell

From the Files of FATE Magazine

The Editors of FATE

2015
Galde Press, Inc.
Lakeville, Minnesota, U.S.A.

The Best of Roswell
© Copyright 2007 by FATE magazine
© Copyright 1959, 1981, 1988, 1990, 1992, 2000, 2003, 2005 by FATE magazine
All rights reserved.
Printed in the United States of America
No part of this book may be used or reproduced in any manner whatsoever without written permission from the publishers except in the case of brief quotations embodied in critical articles and reviews.

First Edition
First Printing, 2007
Second Printing, 2015

Cover painting by Mike Boss

Galde Press, Inc.
PO Box 460
Lakeville, Minnesota 55044–0460

Contents

Introduction, by Richard M. Dolan ix

Keep Your Eye on Venus   Frank Edwards   1
     FATE, August 1959

New Mexico UFO Crash   Jerome Clark   3
     Books: News & Reviews, FATE, February 1981

UFO Crashes: Part III   Jerome Clark   9
     FATE, March 1988

UFO Crashes: Part IV   Jerome Clark   27
     FATE, April 1988

The Fugo Balloons   John Keel   49
     Beyond the Known, FATE, March 1990

The Mystery of S-4   Jerome Clark   57
     UFO Reporter, FATE, June 1990

The Roswell Furor   Stanton Friedman and John Keel   65
     FATE, January 1991

Footnote to Roswell   Jerome Clark   85
     UFO Reporter, FATE, March 1991

Roswell Finale   Stanton Friedman and John Keel   89
     FATE, September 1991

A Tale of Two Crashes   Jerome Clark   103
     UFO Reporter, FATE, November 1992

Return of the Fu-gos   John Keel   109
     Beyond the Known, FATE, April 1993

Roswell Blues (Part I)   J. Antonio Huneeus   117
     UFO Chronicle, FATE, June 1994

Roswell Update (Part II)   J. Antonio Huneeus   125
     UFO Chronicle, FATE, July 1994

The Empire Strikes Back:
     The USAF Roswell Report   J. Antonio Huneeus   133
     UFO Chronicle, FATE, January 1995

New Metallic Artifact   J. Antonio Huneeus   141
     UFO Chronicle, FATE, July 1996

Special Guest Columnist   James E. McWilliams   147
     UFO Chronicle, FATE, July 1997

Roswell UFO Bombshell   Jim Keith   153
     FATE, January 2000

Frank Kaufmann: Roswell Eyewitness?   Kevin D. Randle   157
     FATE, December 2001

Roswell and the Sci-Fi Channel   Kevin D. Randle   173
     FATE, February 2003

Archaeological Site Survey of the Debris Field Kevin D. Randle 187
   FATE, February 2003

Roswell Was Real Rosemary Ellen Guiley 191
   UFO Special, 2005

The Other Paradigm E. A. Guest 197
   FATE, April 2005

Roswell Explained—Again Kevin D. Randle 205
   FATE, September 2005

A Response from Nick Redfern Nick Redfern 217
   FATE, September 2005

Introduction

AS HUMANITY LURCHES ever deeper into the 21st century, into the morass of endless wars, financial ruination, and the daily betrayal of public trust, we see our old ideals, our once optimistic belief in the integrity of "The American Way," slipping farther and farther away. Most people can tell that *something* has gone wrong, that what we thought we knew about our world has been wrong—in a big way.

These days, it's hard to find a traditional, trusting soul: someone who actually believes his or her government will act according to the principles of justice and tell the truth as a matter of policy. Harder still to find someone who doesn't believe that powerful groups would not, given the chance, work secretly together to gain power and money, even if that means breaking the law.

In other words, to engage in a conspiracy.

In such a world, perhaps the craziest thing is that there are still those who laugh at "conspiracy theories." As if governments don't lie, as if corruption of the body politic never occurs.

Indeed, diligent historical research has taught us much about America's "conspiratorial history." It's quite a story, including such noteworthies as the CIA's domestic mail opening programs, the FBI's Cointelpro program, secret military spraying of American cities with biological and chemical agents, the numerous mind control programs, the plutonium injections, the Tuskegee experiments, the use of nerve gas against American defectors in 1970 (Operation Tailwind), good old Watergate, the infamous 1980 October Surprise, CIA complicity in the importation of cocaine by the Nicaraguan Contras. One can run out of breath from such a list, and that only takes us to the 1980s.

These conspiracies are hidden in plain sight. That is, they are freely available to learn about, no one knows about them, and—frequently—no one admits to them. The JFK assassination is the best example of hiding a conspiracy in plain sight. Eighty percent of Americans, and 100 percent of everyone else, believes that President Kennedy was killed in some sort of conspiracy. But without an *official* acknowledgment, e.g. a word from the people who actually run our society, knowledge of what happened by anyone with a brain is apparently not enough to obtain closure, and more importantly justice.

Then there is Roswell. For 30 years after it occurred in 1947, the infamous crash at Roswell was well concealed. The initial press report of a "flying disc" was retracted within three hours, and the Air Force told the world that all the confusion was due to an errant weather balloon. Sorry, folks. Intelligence experts at the 509th Bomb Group couldn't tell the difference between a flying saucer and an ordinary balloon.

Because of the tireless efforts of a few people in the 1970s and 1980s, however, the Roswell story resurfaced, like a body inadequately disposed of. Scores of witnesses and family members were still living, with their story to tell. Their collective story constituted a damning indictment of the lies of America's national security establishment. Not only did it look like UFOs were real—after all, researchers had maintained this for years—but it began to appear that the U.S. military had secretly acquired alien technology and bodies.

It is sometimes easy to forget how radical all this was at the time. Ditto the excitement of uncovering the mystery itself. During the 1980s, when the revelations poured out of Roswell, many investigators believed that the case might be The One that would forever break the secrecy over UFOs. If only enough witnesses were interviewed, if the hardware could be found, or tracked, or described…

That never happened. But the research on Roswell did frighten the Air Force into creating not one but two bogus reports during the 1990s, reports so dense and unreadable—and most importantly *so weak*—that they are tantamount to proof that something important did crash.

Of course, what that object was, this is the question. The debate has been going since the case arose, with no end in sight. Researchers have trotted out every explanation under the stars and sun: ordinary weather balloon, Mogul balloon, Fugo balloon, secret technology acquired from Germany, secret technology acquired from Japan. Oh, yes, and alien spacecraft, whether in the singular or plural.

Most of the of articles in this collection were published over a span of 25 years in the pages of FATE magazine. They provide a vivid picture of the excitement, intrigue, debate, and bitterness provoked by ufology's Holy Grail. They also demonstrate writing and analysis of a high intellectual caliber, enough to show the untutored that the UFO phenomenon deserves the attention of our best minds.

While the exact nature of the crash at Roswell has not been established to everyone's satisfaction, it is not true to say that we have learned nothing. As these articles show, we have learned quite a lot. The authors make it very clear that something very important happened at Roswell in 1947, that the

United States government lied about it for many decades, and that their official explanation to this day remains wholly inadequate, an unfortunate testament to the arrogance of power.

Truth is not relative. It is not the luxury of responsible people to choose what to believe based on personal prejudice or whim. It is rather the obligation of free citizens to *look* for truth. Because it exists, unchanging, independent of outside forces, whether they be popular acclaim or official *diktat*. Roswell may not have delivered all we had hoped for, but the investigation of Roswell was and remains important, not least to demonstrate that truth matters. Now, more than ever, this is something we need to remember.

RICHARD M. DOLAN
Rochester, New York
June 18, 2007

Frank Edwards' Report
Frank Edwards
August 1959

Keep Your Eye on Venus

Note: This short excerpt represents the first mention of Roswell in the pages of FATE—12 years after the fact, but 20 years or more before the incident received national publicity and attention. The main thrust of the article was that we should consider the planet Venus as the origin of the saucers. Edwards had some of the basic facts wrong, such as placing the date of the Roswell crash in 1949 rather than 1947. Other incidents are distorted, thus foreshadowing the confusion and controversy that would follow decades later. However, it is interesting that he also commented on the inept nature of official explanations, a phenomenon which continues to this day.

PERSONALLY I HAVE ALWAYS been skeptical of the official explanation given in connection with a dramatic incident that occurred near Roswell, New Mexico, about 1949. A rancher phoned authorities to report that a huge flying saucer, or something like it, had flashed over his home and crashed on a hillside, tearing itself to bits. The day was clear and sunny so he must have had a reasonably good look at the thing.

A few weeks later, after the customary huddling and considering, Air Force officials released this explanation: It was nothing more than a box kite with a circular metal shield about 18 inches in diameter dangling from it. The photograph of the thing, as carried in many newspapers, showed a man holding a rather bedraggled box kite about four feet tall, complete with shiny bent pie pan attached. It was preposterous to pretend that any normal human being—including that rancher—would not have recognized a crippled box kite floating to earth. Yet the "explanation" was carried on the news services without challenge.

I mention this strange incident, part of a pattern, because conceivably it could have been a case where tangible evidence of a flying saucer might have been obtained. The military promptly took over and after considerable time had elapsed, issued a palpably false statement by way of explanation.

Books: News & Reviews
Jerome Clark
February 1981

New Mexico UFO Crash

O<small>N THE EVENING</small> of July 2, 1947, Mr. and Mrs. Dan Wilmot of Roswell, New Mexico, saw a "big glowing object like two inverted saucers faced mouth to mouth" shoot across the sky from the southeast to the northwest. Six days later Lt. Walter Haut, public information officer at the Roswell Army Air Base, informed the press that base intelligence officer Maj. Jesse A. Marcel had picked up the remains of a flying disk which crashed at an area ranch the week before. The news received international publicity.

What happened? Anyone familiar with the early history of the UFO phenomenon is well aware of the incident. It grew out of a ludicrous misunderstanding, the story goes; the object rancher W. W. Brazel discovered near Corona, New Mexico, on the morning of July 3 and reported three days later was simply a weather device. The material was flown to Carswell Army Air Base in Fort Worth, Texas, where Brig. Gen. Roger M.

Ramey, Commander of the Eighth Air Force, told reporters of the "disk's" true identity.

So the case has been closed for 33 years, remembered only as one of the many mistakes and misidentifications recorded in UFO history. But a new book, *The Roswell Incident* by Charles Berlitz and William L. Moore (Grosset & Dunlap, New York, N.Y., 1980, 168 pages, $10.00), reopens the case and establishes that the object was not a weather device, that everyone who saw it knew it was not, and that it was something very strange indeed. Berlitz and Moore are convinced that the device was part of an extraterrestrial spacecraft, the rest of which went down west of Socorro, New Mexico, on the Plains of San Agustin. When it crashed at San Agustin, it left bodies—humanoid bodies—strewn amid the wreckage.

Moore and ufologist Stanton Friedman, who together conducted the investigation that led to these conclusions, located and interviewed every person who might know something about the Corona recovery. All agreed the "weather device" explanation was a cover story. "The material I saw came from no weather balloon," Marcel states flatly. The late General Ramey's adjutant, Col. Thomas J. DuBose, says the explanation was a fabrication to "put out the fire" and discourage reporters from further prying. The widow of Gen. (then Col.) William Blanchard, at the time of the incident commanding officer of the Roswell base, says her husband knew the object "was nothing made by us…[and] it wasn't Russian either."

Brazel's son Bill, who saw the material and kept some of it until 1949 (when he claims air force officers learned he had it and demanded he surrender it to them), disputes the weather balloon explanation. He declares that his late father was well aware of the phoniness of the official story but kept quiet because the military told him it was his patriotic duty to do so. Other members of the Brazel family confirm this account of what happened.

When Major Marcel came upon the site of the apparent crash, there was, he told Moore, "all kinds of stuff—small beams about three-eighths or a half-inch square with some sort of hieroglyphics on them that nobody could decipher. These looked something like balsa wood and were of about the same weight, except that they were not wood at all. They were very hard, although flexible, and would not burn. There was a great deal of an unusual parchmentlike substance which was brown in color and extremely strong, and a great number of small pieces of a metal like tinfoil, except that it wasn't tinfoil."

The material was flown to Carswell, where Ramey substituted torn-up pieces of an actual weather device for the real material, which was hastily flown to Wright Field in Dayton, Ohio, to be examined secretly. Reporters and photographers, obviously a more credulous lot than their post- Watergate descendants, swallowed whole the official explanation.

This is fascinating stuff, especially to those of us possessed of the will to believe in crashed saucers but unable to make the leap of faith on the strength of the "evidence"—I use the word loosely—usually offered. If it is true that extraordinary claims require extraordinary proof, the sad fact of the matter is that crashed-saucer (CS) advocates from Frank Scully to Len Stringfield have yet to give us anything even vaguely approximating *ordinary* proof. But *The Roswell Incident* provides us with some real evidence, enough certainly to give even the ordinarily skeptical (such as me) pause. At the very least Moore and Friedman (I'll get to Berlitz shortly) have shown that the CS question deserves more than short shrift, all the perfectly sound reasons for rejecting such claims out of hand notwithstanding (among them the perennial but never adequately answered question of how a secret of this magnitude could be kept).

Unfortunately *The Roswell Incident* is a pretty lousy book, in fact about as bad a book as could possibly be written on a subject of such potential importance. Readers of delicate sensibility may not get past the first chapter, which recounts with dogged humorlessness every bogus astronaut UFO report ever to be born in the imaginations of hack writers and immortalized in the pages of the supermarket tabloids. (Late in October 1980 Apollo astronaut Edwin "Buz" Aldrin filed suit against Berlitz, Moore, and Grosset & Dunlap complaining that *Roswell*'s coverage of a fictitious UFO encounter he had on the moon [page 10] damaged his reputation in the scientific community.)

Reportedly written by Berlitz and included at his insistence over the vehement protests of Moore and Friedman, the chapter credits these space age tall tales to "inside sources" whom Berlitz's friend ancient-astronaut theorist Maurice Chatelain supposedly knew "while working for NASA in the 1960s." Since much of the rest of the book cites "inside sources" as its authority, the reader can be excused for waxing skeptical when informed, for example, of a "report from 'an inside source' of what may be the [crashed] 'saucer's' latest stop, at CIA headquarters…'IBM is working on it and they can't figure out how it operates'" (page 107). Uh-huh.

Nor will the informed reader be comforted to read, on page 48, that in 1953 Capt. Edward Ruppelt, recently retired head of Project Blue Book, confided to Mr. and Mrs. Scully that Scully's *Behind the Flying Saucers* (a thoroughly discredited book which contended the government had secretly recovered CSs and Venusian corpses) "was the [book] that gave us the most headaches because it was the closest to the truth." Hogwash.

Ruppelt's private papers (as well as the three chapters appended to the revised 1960 edition of his *Report on Unidentified Flying Objects*) reveal that the late air force investigator didn't believe in *any* kind of UFOs, much less crashed ones. Furthermore, even if there were CSs, Ruppelt, as head of the lowly Blue Book (nothing more than a public relations exercise which did not receive the really sensitive UFO cases), would never have heard about them. And if he had, it's hardly likely that he would blab that fact to the Scullys, of all people.

By the way, Mrs. Scully reveals that her husband's principal informant was not a convicted swindler (*True* magazine's famous exposé to the contrary) but an unnamed "government scientist." Maybe the same one who told Berlitz's friend about the UFOs the astronauts saw on the moon.

Most of *Roswell* never rises above this level of silliness, which I suppose is to be expected since we are dealing, after all, with the man who wrote *The Bermuda Triangle* and whose collected works constitute an irrefutable argument for the contention that you can fool many of the people much of the time. (And Berlitz, once he figures he's onto something, never lets go. One of the officers involved in the Roswell episode, we learn, "was later lost when his plane mysteriously vanished over the Bermuda Triangle.") From page 92 to the end the book does little more than recite arcane (and completely unverified) saucer anecdotes, linking them with such connecting phrases as "if this rumor is true," "reported from 'an inside source'" and so on.

One of my all-time favorite saucer folktales is the subject of Chapter Seven, in which we learn (or are reminded; this one went the rounds back in the 1950s) of the day Ike got to see the crashed saucer. The rest of the world naively thought he was getting a tooth capped in Palm Springs, California—an obviously ridiculous story, we are told, because 25 years later a member of the dentist's family "cannot recall" the details of the dental work. The chief informant is one Gerald Light, about whom nothing is known except that once he wrote California occultist Meade Layne to report that President Eisenhower "was spirited over the Muroc (Air Force Base) during his visit to Palm Springs recently." After the reprinted letter ends, the test resumes with "Assuming that this letter is not a hoax…" One doesn't know whether to laugh or weep.

Torn between Moore's skilled investigative journalism and Berlitz's hackwork, Roswell lapses into deep schizophrenia, nearly taking the reader along.

I don't know what kind of object the air force recovered at Corona. My instinct tells me it could not have been a UFO, but I don't know what else it could have been. Berlitz and Moore attempt to connect the incident, as I've already mentioned, with an alleged crash west of Socorro, where one day in June or July 1947 engineer Barney Barnett supposedly found wreckage and humanoid bodies. Barnett died in 1969 and Moore got his story from friends and business associates to whom he had related it years earlier and who say Barnett was a truthful man not given to yarn-spinning.

Barnett claimed members of a University of Pennsylvania archaeological team (which Moore has established was working in the area at the time) also saw the remains. Military personnel soon arrived at the site and sent them away with instructions never to tell anyone what they had seen.

Unless these additional witnesses come forward (and the fact that none has in all these years is hardly grounds for confidence), the Socorro story must remain just another unverified CS report. But the Corona incident is something else—a fascinating and perplexing episode. It deserves a far better book than *The Roswell Incident.*

UFO Crashes: Part III
For 40 years the U.S. government has kept silent about the most important UFO case of all.

Jerome Clark
March 1988

It rates a mere three paragraphs in Ted Bloecher's comprehensive *Report on the UFO Wave of 1947* (1967), where it is listed under the heading "Hoaxes and Mistakes."

The incident, which Bloecher characterizes as an "embarrassingly obvious mistake," occurred in early July of that year. As Bloecher tells it, "a farmer named Brazell [sic] discovered a 'disc' on his ranch at Corona. After hearing news broadcasts of flying saucer reports, Brazell, who had stored the 'disc' in a barn, notified the Sheriff's Office in Roswell, who in turn notified Maj. Jesse A. Marcel, of the Roswell Army Air Field intelligence office. The 'disc' was taken to Roswell Field for examination. Through a series of clumsy blunders in public relations, and a desire by the press to manufacture a crashed disc if none would obligingly crash of itself, the story got blown up out of all proportion in headlines that read 'Crashed Disc Found in New Mexico.'"

In reality, Bloecher writes, the "disc" was composed of tinfoil and was the wreckage of a "high altitude weather device." The matter was cleared up when the material was flown to Eighth Air Force headquarters in Fort Worth, Texas, and Brig. Gen. Roger M. Ramey announced the mundane truth to assembled reporters.

Bloecher's account of what happened is based entirely on newspaper stories from the period.

***

On September 15, 1950, members of the Canadian embassy staff were participating in a routine meeting in the Washington office of American physicist Robert Sarbacher. Dr. Sarbacher, a member of the Defense Department's Research and Development Board, was an impressively credentialed professional: a graduate of the University of Florida (1933), Princeton (1934), and Harvard (Sc.D., 1939), a Harvard instructor in physics and communications engineering (1936-40), a professor of electrical engineering at the Illinois Institute of Technology (1940–42), a visiting professor at Harvard (1941), a wartime scientific consultant to the navy (1942–45), a dean of the graduate school of the Georgia Institute of Technology (1945–49), an inventor, an author of technical works such as *Hyper and Ultra-High Frequency Engineering* (1944), head of his own business and member of a number of corporate boards. In 1950 he was one of a number of accomplished businessmen and scientists serving as "dollar-a-year men"—volunteers providing their time and expertise to the Defense Department.

There was nothing unusual about the meeting. Sarbacher and the embassy personnel got together periodically to discuss matters of concern to the national security of their countries. Typically these related to Sarbacher's specialty, the technical problems associated with guided-missile control. But the conversations often dealt with other matters as well.

On this late-summer day the Canadians were curious about claims made in a best-selling book, *Behind the Flying Saucers*, by entertainment columnist Frank Scully. Was it true, they asked, that the U.S. government possessed the remains of crashed flying discs and their dead occupants?

Yes, it was, Sarbacher said. A November 21, 1950, memo prepared by W. B. Smith, a senior radio engineer with the Canadian government's Department of Transport, summarized Sarbacher's reply:

a. The matter is the most highly classified subject in the United States Government, rating higher even than the H-bomb.

b. Flying saucers exist.

c. Their modus operandi is unknown but concentrated effort is being made by a small group headed by Doctor Vannevar Bush.

d. The entire matter is considered by the United States authorities to be of tremendous significance.

In 1950, as now, the public position of the U.S. government was that UFOs were all explainable, or potentially explainable, as misinterpreted conventional phenomena and hoaxes. Smith was sufficiently impressed by what he heard to urge the Canadian government to set up a UFO project, which it did soon afterwards, under the code name Magnet, under Smith's direction.

The Smith memo was classified Top Secret until 1969, when it was downgraded to Confidential. In 1978, when Canadian ufologist Arthur Bray secured a copy from his government, he began an investigation, hoping to learn just who Smith's source had been (Sarbacher's name is not mentioned in the memo, nor is the date of the meeting). Bray eventually gained access to the late W. B. Smith's notes and got the information he was looking for.

The notes purport to recount the conversation word for word. At one point Smith asks, "Do they come from another planet?" Sarbacher replies, "All we know is, we didn't make them, and it's pretty certain they didn't originate on the earth."

"Is there any way in which I can get more information?" Smith says.

"I suppose you could be cleared through your own Defense Department," Sarbacher says, "and I am pretty sure arrangements could be made to exchange information. If you have anything to contribute, we would be glad to talk it over, but I can't give you any more at the present time."

So far as anyone knows, that was the last Smith ever heard about the Ultimate Secret, at least from a U.S. government source.

In 1982 Bray reported all this to the annual conference of the Mutual UFO Network. In due course—specifically, when investigator William Steinman found Sarbacher's name and three-inch, tiny-print entry in *Who's Who in America*—it was learned that he was still alive and living in Florida. Steinman wrote him and on November 29, 1983, Sarbacher responded.

Sarbacher said he remembered the meeting at which UFOs were discussed and confirmed that he had said what the memo indicated he had said. He wrote, "My association with the Research and Development Board...was rather limited so that although I had been invited to participate in several discussions associated with the reported recoveries, I could not personally attend the meetings.... Naturally, I was more familiar with the subject matter under discussion, at that time. Actually, I would have been able to give more specific answers had I attended the meetings concerning the subject. You must understand that I took this assignment as a private contribution.... My first responsibility was the maintenance of my own business activity so that my participation was limited.

"About the only thing I remember at this time is that certain materials reported to have come from flying saucer crashes were extremely light and very tough. I am sure our laboratories analyzed them very carefully.

"There were reports that instruments or people operating these machines were also of very light weight, sufficient to withstand the tremendous deceleration and acceleration associated with their machinery. I remember in talking with some of the people at the office that I got the impression these 'aliens' were constructed like certain insects we have observed on earth, wherein because of the low mass the inertial forces involved in operation of these instruments would be quite low.

"I still do not know why the high order of classification has been given and why the denial of the existence of these devices."

On January 17, 1985, unsure of what to make of all this, I called Sarbacher and talked with him for about an hour. During my long association with UFO study I had heard a lot of wild, unverifiable stories about crashed discs and I had long been skeptical. Many tellers of such tales had proven to be pathological liars, nobodies trying to make themselves seem like somebodies by pretending to be privy to the Ultimate Secret. But Sarbacher certainly didn't seem to be one of these. Before I called, I'd spent time in the library finding out what I could about him. It was not clear to me what the author of a book such as the *Encyclopedic Dictionary of Electronics and Nuclear Engineering* had to gain by telling falsehoods about crashed UFOs, especially in the official position he occupied in 1950.

Sarbacher turned out to be friendly but apologetic, saying that all this had happened so long ago that he just couldn't remember much of it. Yes, colleagues and friends such as Vannevar Bush (President Truman's chief science advisor) and mathematician John von Neumann were involved and they had told him about the recovered vehicles, which were believed to be from another solar system. He said that on one occasion he was invited to attend a conference at Wright-Patterson Air Force Base where Air Force personnel were to discuss what they had concluded to date from their analysis of the recovered material. Unfortunately, owing to pressing other business, Sarbacher did not go but did talk with those who did.

Mostly, however, Sarbacher could not recall important details such as where the UFOs had come down. He said he had not been personally involved in the UFO project and his own attention had been focused on matters of more pressing concern to him, such as guided-missile control. Aside from hearing about the recoveries, seeing some of the official documents, and being invited to attend a conference, his own involvement was confined to being taken to sites where ground had been scorched following a UFO landing. He said that he and his colleagues were asked to examine the traces from the perspectives of their various areas of expertise and to see what they could learn. Sarbacher could not recall where these sites were.

I remarked that he seemed awfully blase for a man who knew something that many people would regard as extraordinary. Sarbacher allowed as how this was probably so but said his life had been a busy one, with many responsibilities and interests, and essentially the UFO aspect was something he really had not been able to pursue or even give a great deal of thought to. He told me he had never read a book on the subject and I determined that he didn't even know the name of the Air Force's UFO project, Blue Book.

Sarbacher, unlike others who had told me about the Ultimate Secret, seemed entirely straightforward and honest. When he didn't remember something, which was often, he answered my questions by saying, "I don't know." He treated the entire matter simply as a curiosity, not as some big truth to which he as someone important was privy. In fact, he was disarmingly modest. "I wish I could refer you to someone who was more directly involved than I was," he said. "Unfortunately they're all long gone."

Sarbacher was reluctant to speculate even when I encouraged him to do so. "I don't know why this is still a secret," he said. "Maybe it was the [Orson] Welles ['Invasion from Mars'] broadcast — people get excited and their imagination runs away. [The government] didn't seem to want anyone to believe vehicles from interstellar space were here. I don't think the whole thing's unraveled yet."

Ufologists and fellow physicists Bruce Maccabee and Stanton Friedman (Friedman spent part of a day with Sarbacher on the latter's yacht) heard precisely the same story. He neither elaborated on it nor contradicted himself. He related the story only when asked to do so and he did not act in any way like a man who was trying to draw attention to himself— not that someone of his considerable professional accomplishments had any need to do so. Invariably modest about his limited role in the matter, he declined invitations to speak publicly at UFO conferences or other forums. In short, if Sarbacher had been talking about anything but the Ultimate Secret, it would not have occurred to anybody to think he was lying.

It was my impression—and the impression of all others who spoke with him—that Sarbacher (who died in the summer of 1986) was telling the truth as he understood it. No other explanation makes sense. In any case, by now there is a great deal of independent evidence to suggest that, beneath all the lies and fantasies about crashed discs, there is an Ultimate Secret and it is very much like the one Sarbacher described.

***

In January 1978 the most important investigation in the history of civilian UFO research began. William L. Moore, a schoolteacher and aspiring writer from Herman, Minnesota, and Stanton T. Friedman, a nuclear physicist with a long professional resume and a longtime interest in the UFO phenomenon, were eating pizza in a Morris, Minnesota, restaurant and discussing some odd rumors they'd been hearing—rumors that, if true, would turn an obscure incident from three decades earlier into the most crucial case of all time. If what they were hearing had any foundation, all of UFO history would have to be rewritten. And although they had no inkling of it then, the investigation on which they were about to embark would change their own lives forever.

The first hint that what would be called the "Roswell incident" was more than a silly misunderstanding about a weather balloon had come two or three years earlier, when a California forest ranger told the late Bobbi Ann Gironda, a writer interested in UFOs, that his mother had had an interesting UFO experience in New Mexico. When Gironda and Friedman interviewed her, the woman, Lydia Sleppy, told a strange story.

She said that at four o'clock in the afternoon of July 7, 1947, as she was operating the teletype at radio station KOAT in Albuquerque, she got a phone call from Johnny McBoyle, reporter and part owner of sister station KSWS in Roswell. KSWS had no teletype of its own but used KOAT's when it had something it wanted to go out.

McBoyle was excited. He reported that one of those flying saucers everyone had been talking about had crashed near Roswell. He'd been out there and seen it. It looked like a "big crumpled dishpan." The army was there and was going to pick it up. "And get this," he added. "They're saying something about little men being on board…. Start getting this on the teletype right away while I'm on the phone."

Sleppy began typing as McBoyle dictated the story to her. A few sentences later the teletype stopped. Assuming there was a mechanical problem, Sleppy told McBoyle what had happened. McBoyle suddenly seemed distracted. From what she could overhear, it sounded as if he were talking with someone else. Then he said to her in a strained voice, "Wait a minute, I'll get back to you." At that moment the teletype resumed working. Now it was spelling out a message apparently directed to Sleppy: "ATTENTION ALBUQUERQUE: DO NOT TRANSMIT. REPEAT DO NOT TRANSMIT THIS MESSAGE. STOP COMMUNICATION IMMEDIATELY."

Astonished, Sleppy informed McBoyle of what she was seeing. McBoyle replied tersely, "Forget about it. You never heard it. Look, you're not supposed to know. Don't talk about it to anyone."

When Friedman located McBoyle and asked him about the episode, McBoyle said, "Forget about it…. It never happened."

On January 20, 1978, Friedman lectured on UFOs at the University of Louisiana. While promoting the lecture at a local television station, he was introduced to the manager who casually suggested he talk with Maj. Jesse Marcel. Marcel, he said, had actually handled a UFO "way back." He'd known Marcel a long time because of their mutual interest in ham radio.

Friedman called Marcel who claimed that while in the Army Air Force he picked up a great quantity of material from a crashed UFO near Roswell. He couldn't recall exactly when it happened but it had been a long time ago.

Marcel sounded sincere but Friedman, having heard his share of unsubstantiated tales of the Ultimate Secret, wasn't entirely convinced.

Still, he was intrigued and as he and Moore discussed these two stories, putting them into the context of the curiously persistent rumors of the Ultimate Secret, they decided that an investigation was worthwhile. After all, this time they had some real names. Typically Ultimate Secret stories were second- or thirdhand or the informants were anonymous and untraceable.

Before they were through eight years later, Friedman and Moore had located and interviewed 92 persons who knew something about the Roswell incident. Thirty of these were individuals directly involved with the discovery, recovery, or cover-up of the object. Thirty-three were family members, friends, or neighbors of the direct witnesses; Friedman and Moore interviewed them as a way of checking the reliability of the firsthand informants. The other 29 informants provided useful background information.

The names of most of these informants are on the public record. Some have been interviewed by newspaper reporters and network-television journalists (most prominently on ABC-TV's popular *Night-line*). Their stories are consistent and the accuracy of their testimony has never been seriously challenged. The Roswell incident, for all its mindboggling implications, is one of the best-documented cases in UFO history. If the informants are not radically mistaken about what they observed and experienced, these conclusions seem inevitable: UFOs are extraterrestrial spacecraft and the U.S. government has known that, and covered it up, for more than four decades.

A full account of the Roswell incident, complete with voluminous documentation, is impossible here because of space limitations. What follows is a summary of the story that emerges from the testimony of the 92 informants:

A glowing object which looked, in the witnesses' words, "like two inverted saucers faced mouth to mouth" flew over Roswell, New Mexico, at 9:50 p.m. on July 2, 1947, and was observed by Mr. and Mrs. Dan Wilmot. The disc, which came from the southeast, was moving in a northwestern direction—where, 75 miles later, near the small town of Corona, lay a sheep ranch managed by one W. W. ("Mac") Brazel.

That evening an electrical storm erupted in the Corona area. Sometime late in the evening Brazel and two of his younger children, Paul and Bessie (his wife lived in Tularosa and an older son, Bill, was married and living in Lincoln County, New Mexico), heard something that sounded like a loud explosion. The explosion was peculiar; it was, Bill Brazel would recall his father had told him, "different from ordinary thunder. "Still, the Brazels assumed it was just part of the storm. It was not until the next morning that another interpretation occurred to them.

That morning, when he went out to check on the sheep, Brazel found the wreckage of some kind of aircraft scattered over a band a quarter mile long and several hundred feet wide. The vehicle seemed to have exploded. Brazel thought immediately of the sound he had heard late the previous evening.

The next day Brazel picked up some of the material and brought it to the house. In the evening he visited his nearest neighbor, Floyd Proctor, and invited him to come over and look at the material, which he described as the "strangest stuff I've ever seen." Proctor wasn't interested but Brazel, intensely curious, decided to ask around and see if anyone knew where it came from. The following night Brazel, who had no phone, drove to Corona and spoke with his brother-in-law Hollis Wilson and another man. There for the first time he heard of the "flying saucers" that people in New Mexico and elsewhere had been reporting for the past two weeks. Wilson and the other man thought that maybe one had crashed on the Brazel ranch.

Brazel had his doubts about the flying-saucer explanation but he had to admit he'd never seen anything like this material before. He had already planned to go to Roswell to buy a new Jeep, so he decided that while he was doing that, he would take some of the material to the sheriff's office.

In the morning he drove down to Tularosa, where he left the two children with their mother, and continued on to Roswell.

***

When the sheriff's office phoned Roswell Field to report Brazel's discovery, Maj. Jesse Marcel, ranking staff officer in charge of intelligence, was eating lunch at the officers' club. He was instructed to interview Brazel. After talking with the rancher, he became convinced that something important had happened and so informed the base commanding officer, Col. William H. Blanchard. The two officers agreed the material was probably from a downed aircraft.

An hour later Marcel, Brazel, and a Counter-intelligence Corps (CIC) agent named "Cav" Cavitt drove in separate vehicles to the crash site. In a 1979 interview Marcel described what they found:

There was all kinds of stuff—small beams about 3/8ths or a half-inch square with some sort of hieroglyphics on them that nobody could decipher. These looked something like balsa wood and were of about the same weight, although flexible, and would not burn. There was a great deal of an unusual parchmentlike substance which was brown in color and extremely strong, and a great number of small pieces of a metal like tinfoil, except that it wasn't tinfoil. I was interested in electronics and kept looking for something that resembled instruments or electronic equipment, but I didn't find anything. One of the other fellows, Cavitt, I think, found a black, metallic-looking box several inches square....

[The parchment material] had little numbers and symbols that we had to call hieroglyphics because I could not understand them. They could not be read, they were just like symbols, something that meant something, and they were not all the same, but the same general pattern, I would say. They were pink and purple. They looked like they were painted on. These little numbers could not be broken, could not be burned. I even took my cigarette lighter and tried to burn the material we found that resembled parchment and balsa, but it would not burn—wouldn't even smoke.

The metal, Marcel recalled, was as thin as the foil in a pack of cigarettes and weighed practically nothing. But it could not be bent, or even dented, with a 16-pound sledgehammer. Nor could it be torn or cut. "It was possible to flex this stuff back and forth, even to wrinkle it, but you could not put a crease in it that would stay.... I would almost have to describe it as a metal with plastic properties," he said.

Readers will recall Sarbacher's remark that "certain materials reported to have come from flying saucer crashes were extremely light and very tough."

Others who saw the material remembered it much the same way. Mac Brazel's daughter Bessie recalled it looks like "a sort of aluminum-like foil...very light in weight." William Brazel said it was "something on the order of tinfoil except that [it] wouldn't tear.... You could wrinkle it and lay it back down and it immediately resumed its original shape...quite pliable.... Almost like a plastic, but definitely metallic in nature. Dad once said that the Army [Air Force] had once told him it was not anything made by us." Bill Rickett, a CIC agent based in Roswell, remembered the material was "very strong and very light.... As far as I know, no one ever figured out what it was made of." Walt Whitmore, Jr., who saw some of the material when his father, owner of Roswell radio station KGFL, brought Brazel to his home, stated it was "very much like lead foil in appearance but could not be torn or cut at all... extremely light in weight."

Bessie Brazel added, "Some of these pieces had something like numbers and lettering on them, but there were no words we were able to make out. [When these] were held up to the light they showed what looked like pastel flowers or designs.... The figures were written out like you would write numbers in columns...but they didn't look like the numbers we use at all. What gave me the idea they were numbers...was the way they were all ranged out in colors." According to Walt Whitmore, Jr., "Some of the material had a sort of writing on it which looked like numbers which had either been added or multiplied (i.e. in columns)."

* * *

By now the story was a national sensation. When Marcel and Cavitt returned from the Brazel ranch, with their cars full of the material, reporters knew of the alleged flying-disc crash. Lt. Walter Haut, public-information officer at Roswell Field, had already alerted Associated Press.

The next day, the 8th, Lieutenant Haut issued a press release:

The many rumors regarding the flying disc became a reality yesterday when the intelligence office of the 509th Bomb Group of the Eighth Air Force, Roswell Army Air Field, was fortunate enough to gain possession of a disc through the cooperation of one of the local ranchers and the sheriff's office of Chaves County.

The flying object landed on a ranch near Roswell sometime last week. Not having phone facilities, the rancher stored the disc until such time as he was able to contact the sheriff's office, who in turn notified Major Jesse A. Marcel of the 509th Bomb Group Intelligence Office.

Action was immediately taken and the disc was picked up at the rancher's home. It was inspected at the Roswell Army Air Field and subsequently loaned by Major Marcel to higher headquarters.

Soon afterwards Colonel Blanchard found himself at the receiving end of what the *Washington Post* described as a "blistering rebuke" from his superiors, Eighth Air Force Commander Brig. Gen. Roger M. Ramey and Deputy Air Force Chief Lt. Gen. Hoyt S. Vandenberg, who were furious about the press release. They told him they wanted the material shipped immediately to Eighth Air Force Headquarters (now Carswell AFB) in Fort Worth,

Texas. So Blanchard ordered Marcel to load the material aboard a B-29 and deliver it to General Ramey. From there it was to be flown, with Marcel again watching over it, to Wright Field in Dayton, Ohio, where it would be analyzed.

When Marcel got to Fort Worth, General Ramey ordered him not to talk with reporters. Then Ramey called in the press and announced that the "disc" was really just a weather balloon. As proof he displayed a weather balloon and brought in the base weather officer, Irving Newton, to identify it as such. Newton would recall that the balloon material was "very flimsy—you would have to be careful not to tear it—unlike the material at Roswell. Nonetheless reporters were asked to believe that the balloon and the "flying saucer" were one and the same. Since the object was known to be nothing out of the ordinary, there was no reason to do anything further with it.

In fact, the real material was, in the words of a Dallas FBI teletype message sent that evening to J. Edgar Hoover in Washington, "being transported to Wright Field by special plane for examination." Marcel was not aboard. He was sent back to Roswell and warned to say nothing more. As he would tell Moore many years later, "The cover story about the balloon [was] just to get the press off [Ramey's] back. The press was told it was just a balloon and that the flight to Wright was canceled; but all that really happened was that I was removed from the flight and someone else took it to Wright."

According to retired Air Force Brig. Gen. Thomas J. DuBose, who in July 1947 served as adjutant to General Ramey's staff in Fort Worth, the order to effect a cover-up using a phony balloon identification came directly from the Pentagon, specifically from Gen. Clements McMullen. There were, DuBose said, "orders from on high to ship the material…directly to Wright Field by plane."

CIC officer Rickett stated flatly, "The Air Force's explanation that it was a balloon was totally untrue. It was not a balloon. I never did know for sure exactly what its purpose was but it wasn't ours."

Only those who had not seen the material were fooled. The late Colonel Blanchard's former wife Emily Simms recalled, "At first he thought it might be Russian because of the strange symbols on it. Later on, he realized it wasn't Russian either."

***

Meanwhile in Roswell, radio station owner W. E. Whitmore, who had interviewed Brazel and recorded his account, tried to get the story on the Mutual Network wire but couldn't get through. When he began broadcasting preliminary accounts on KFGL, he received a long-distance person-to-person call from a man who identified himself as the head of the Federal Communications Commission in Washington, D.C. The caller warned Whitmore that the matter he was discussing involved national security and that if he wanted to keep his license he would drop the story and forget all about it. No sooner had the caller hung up than the phone rang again. This time it was U.S. Senator Chavez of New Mexico, chairman of the Senate Appropriations Committee, telling Whitmore he had better do as the FCC director said. He did.

That morning Counter-intelligence Corps officers Cavitt and Rickett and one other man had driven to the Brazel ranch and enlisted Brazel in an effort to recover more pieces of the wreckage. The crash site was being guarded by armed military policemen who were sending reporters and curiosity-seekers away. The four returned to Roswell in two vehicles (Brazel drove his own pickup) and in due course Brazel went his own way, with the understanding that he was to meet Cavitt the next morning. At the base the officers were informed that because of the press release all hell had broken loose and they had better get Brazel before matters got even further out of hand. A frantic search found the rancher at Whitmore's home.

Brazel was taken and held incommunicado for a week. He surfaced only on two occasions, both of them on the 8th, when Brazel, accompanied by agent Cavitt, appeared at the office of the *Roswell Daily Record* and at the KGFL studio. In each case he told (under what all surviving members of his family, Cavitt's assistant Rickett, and two local reporters all have described as duress) the story that the Army Air Force was now circulating: that the object was only a balloon.

The next day the *Daily Record*, taking the account at face value, headlined its story "Harassed Rancher Who Located 'Saucer' Sorry He Told About it."

But at KGFL newsman Frank Joyce had his doubts. He had been the first reporter to hear the story. On the 6th he had called the sheriff's office on other business just when Brazel was reporting his discovery. Sheriff Wilcox suggested Joyce might want to talk with him and he did, but the reporter, not knowing what to make of the story, did nothing about it. Only when he got Haut's press release two days later did he realize he had missed a scoop. And when he heard Brazel's new version, he recognized it as significantly different from the first one.

Members of the Brazel family long remembered their father's bitterness (he died in 1965) about how he had been treated. The entire family was warned not to discuss the incident. "Back in those days," Bessie Brazel recalled, "when the military told you not to talk about something, it wasn't discussed."

The elder Brazel went to his grave without ever telling all he knew, even to family members. During his detention the Air Force sent soldiers to the site to collect every scrap of the material they could find. Aerial reconnaissance was conducted and both air and surface photographs were taken. One of those who participated, C. E. Zerbe, recalled in 1983 that the films were not processed at Roswell Field. "Everything was sent out by special plane for processing elsewhere, possibly at Fort Worth. I never knew for sure."

The only evidence that remained was in the hands of Brazel's son Bill. As he would relate years later, "The Air Force had a whole platoon of men out there picking up every piece and shred they could find. Still, every time I rode through that particular pasture I would make a point to look. Seems like every time after a good rain I would manage to find a piece or two that they had overlooked. After about a year and a half or two years I had managed to accumulate quite a small collection—about enough that if you were to lay it out on this tabletop it would take up about as much area as [a] briefcase."

Then one night in 1949 Bill Brazel visited a watering hole in Corona.

As the evening progressed his tongue got looser and in due course he was talking about his collection of flying-saucer artifacts. The next morning a staff car from Roswell Field showed up and four soldiers, a captain, and three enlisted men, came to his door. They wanted to see his collection.

After he had shown it to the military men, the captain said the material related to national security and Bill Brazel would have to surrender it.

"I didn't know what else to do," Bill Brazel related, "so I agreed. Next he wanted me to take them out to the pasture where I had found this stuff.... After they had poked around a bit and satisfied themselves that there didn't appear to be any more of the material out there…the captain…said that if I ever found any more it was most important that I call him at Roswell right away. Naturally I said I would but I never did because after that I never found any more."

UFO Crashes: Part IV

Behind the UFO cover-up, say intelligence officers, is the deepest secret of all: contact with beings from another solar system.

Jerome Clark
April 1988

What was the object that crashed near Corona, New Mexico, in early July 1947? No fewer than 10 of the 30 firsthand witnesses interviewed by William L. Moore and Stanton T. Friedman identified the object as a spacecraft. The others say simply that they have no idea what it was. The material that the officers from Roswell Field recovered was reported to be unlike anything used, then or now, in the construction of aircraft, balloons or guided missiles.

Non-UFO explanations for the object that figures in what is called the "Roswell incident" have been offered, but subsequent investigation has failed to substantiate them. Some theorists have proposed that the object was a Skyhook balloon, part of the secret U.S. Navy Skyhook project to conduct tests in the upper atmosphere. In fact, the first Skyhook balloon was launched from Camp Ripley, Minnesota, *five months after* the Roswell crash.

A number of balloon experiments were conducted in the Southwest in 1947, but such balloons were familiar to local people, both military and civilian, and would not have been mistaken for something so extraordinary as the Roswell craft. When Gen. Roger Ramey, Commander of the Eighth Air Force, showed base weather officer Irving Newton a balloon and claimed it was the object recovered at Roswell, Newton was surprised that the Roswell people hadn't recognized it. "It was a regular Rawin sonde," he recalled. "They must have seen hundreds of them. " Two weather-balloon crashes occurred around the same time, not in New Mexico but in Ohio, and the military had no trouble identifying the devices, which did not have to be sent on to "higher headquarters" as was the case at Roswell.

Classified rocket experiments (using V-2s) took place at Fort Bliss in El Paso, Texas, on June 12 and July 3 but in both cases the missiles were recovered.

In early September Gen. George F. Schulgen, Deputy Assistant Chief of Air Staff-2, sent FBI Director J. Edgar Hoover a classified memo which stated that "a complete survey of research activities discloses that the Army Air Forces has no project with the characteristics similar to those which have been associated with the flying discs."

There is, however, another element to the story—one that, if true, conclusively proves the Roswell craft's nonearthly origin. If there were bodies of the vehicle's occupants and these bodies were not of human beings, no one could dispute that the remains that rancher Mac Brazel discovered and the Army Air Force recovered soon afterwards were of a spaceship from another planet.

The Brazels, Maj. Jesse Marcel (who led the initial recovery operation), and Lt. Walter Haut say there were no bodies. At least they saw no bodies, they say, in what they were able to examine of the wreckage.

Conrad Zerbe, a photographer who participated in aerial reconnaissance of the crash area, says there were bodies. They were discovered from the air some distance from the wreckage of their presumed craft. To all appearances the occupants had bailed out of the vehicle in an unsuccessful attempt to survive the crash.

Frank Joyce, then a reporter for Roswell radio station KGFL, now a well-known news broadcaster in the Southwest, claims to know from first-hand observation that there were bodies, but he refuses to discuss the subject publicly.

When Friedman asked Bill Rickett, a Counter-Intelligence Corps agent who participated in the investigation, if there were bodies, he was struck by the retired officer's response. According to Friedman, Rickett "indicated that this was an area he couldn't talk about. He indicated there were different levels of security about this work—that a directive had come down placing this at a high level. He went on to say that certain subjects were discussed only in rooms that couldn't be bugged."

On July 7, 1947, Lydia Sleppy, who worked for Albuquerque radio station KOAT, took a call from reporter Johnny McBoyle of sister station KSWS in Roswell. McBoyle wanted to get a story on the press wires about the crashed disc. He had been to the site and seen it and, he told Sleppy, "They're saying something about little men being on board...." At that point McBoyle stopped talking and would say no more, apparently warned to keep silent. Three and a half decades later he still would not talk about the incident. (For more details see Part III.)

Many years later military and intelligence personnel would separately tell a UFO investigator and several individuals in the media that the remains of four humanoid bodies were found in the general area of the Roswell crash. The beings were about four feet tall and had gray skins, large heads, and oversized slanted eyes. Their hairless bodies were thin and there were four long fingers on each hand. Later, the sources said, the U.S. government would give them a name: the "Grays." And it would come to know them well—at least as well as one race can know another which is unimaginably different from itself.

* * *

In late July 1947 an anonymous Air Force officer prepared an evaluation of the UFO question as it looked one month after Kenneth Arnold's sighting on June 24. He reviewed 18 of the best sightings, including Arnold's, and concluded that "this flying saucer situation is not all imaginary or seeing too much in some natural phenomenon." He noted that according to reliable reports the objects appeared "metallic." They had a circular or disc or elliptical shape, were flat on the bottom and domed on the top, and sometimes flew in formation.

Everything indicated that this was a phenomenon of great importance, something of both scientific and national-security interest. So why did there seem to be so little interest at the highest levels of the U.S. government? The officer thought he had an answer: "Lack of topside inquiries, when compared to the prompt and demanding enquiries that have originated topside upon former events, give more than ordinary weight to the possibility that this is a project about which the President, etc., know."

On October 20, 1969, in an internal Air Force memo which came to light some years later as part of a release of UFO documents under the Freedom of Information Act, Brig. Gen. C. H. Bolender noted that "reports [of UFOs]...which could affect national security...are not part of the Blue Book system...[and are] handled through the standard Air Force procedures designed for this purpose."

Between these two memos stretched a long and mostly sorry history of apparent Air Force mishandling of UFO reports.

The formal—or at least public—Air Force investigation began on December 30, 1947, when Maj. Gen. L. C. Craigie ordered the establishment of Project Sign, to be headquartered at Wright Field (now Wright-Patterson Air Force Base) under the Technical Intelligence Division of the Air Materiel Command. It would carry a 2A restricted classification (lA was the highest) and would "collect, collate, evaluate, and distribute to interested government agencies and contractors all information concerning sightings and phenomena in the atmosphere which can be construed to be of concern to the national security."

Project Sign began work on January 22, 1948. In the next few months Sign personnel found no evidence that UFOs were Russian, American, or imaginary. That left open a disturbing possibility: that they came from somewhere other than the earth. A July 24 sighting, in which two Eastern Air Lines pilots flying over Alabama reported a near-collision with a huge cigar-shaped object with two rows of lighted windows and an orange flame shooting from its rear, clinched Sign's growing belief that the planet was being visited.

They prepared a top-secret "Estimate of the Situation," which argued that flying saucers were real and interplanetary. Their report was delivered through channels to Air Force Chief of Staff Gen. Hoyt S. Vandenberg, who rejected it and sent it back. A few months later all known copies were burned. None has surfaced since.

Soon the pro-extraterrestrial group at Sign fell into disfavor and others, who believed UFOs to be explainable in conventional terms, assumed control of the project, which in late 1948 was renamed Grudge, initiating what Capt. Edward J. Ruppelt would call the "Dark Ages."

Grudge personnel were determined to destroy the flying-saucer phenomenon at any cost. They conducted only perfunctory investigations and produced forced or unlikely "conventional" explanations of sightings. When Grudge released its final report publicly on December 27, 1949, it declared that "all evidence and analysis indicated that UFOs were the result of misinterpretation of various conventional objects," hoaxes, hysteria or mental illness.

The Air Force announced that it was closing Grudge. In fact, Grudge was not closed, only (in historian David M. Jacobs' words) "in a state of suspended animation." By the summer of 1951 its personnel at Air Materiel Command headquarters consisted of one lieutenant. One of Grudge's projects, Twinkle (dealing with reports of unexplained "green fireballs" in the Southwest), continued but was classified.

In September 1951, following spectacular radar-visual sightings of structured metallic discs over Fort Monmouth, New Jersey, the Air Force decided to reorganize Grudge under the direction of Capt. Ed Ruppelt of the Air Technical Intelligence Center (ATIC), formerly the Intelligence Division of the Air Materiel Command. Determined to conduct an open-minded inquiry, which he knew Grudge had not done, he removed hard-core anti-UFO elements and let it be known that his investigators were to be advocates of no UFO theory, pro or con.

Ruppelt reorganized the project, now called Blue Book, brought in trained personnel and saw to it that reports were investigated in a professional manner. The persistence of puzzling, well-documented sightings gave rise again to speculation within the project that UFOs were of extraterrestrial origin. In 1956, when he wrote his memoirs of his Blue Book experiences (*The Report on Unidentified Flying Objects*), he treated the subject with admirable balance, but no one who read it could doubt that he considered extraterrestrial visitation distinctly possible.

An outbreak of sightings over Washington, D.C., in July 1952 caused so much alarm that the White House directed that a scientific advisory panel consider the UFO question. The CIA was put in charge of the project and in early January 1953 the panel, whose membership consisted of prominent scientists under the direction of physicist H. P. Robertson, met for three days, between the 14th and the 17th. It listened to briefings from Blue Book and other military investigators, looked over some of the reports, and decided there was nothing to them. As one panel member, astrophysicist Thornton Page, would recall, the group "tended to ignore the five or ten percent of UFO reports that are highly reliable and have not as yet been explained." At the time, Page recalls, he felt the subject was "ludicrous" (an opinion shared by other members of the panel; S. A. Goudsmit, for example, considered UFOs a "complete waste of time"), although in later years Page would develop a serious interest in the UFO phenomenon.

The Robertson panel urged that UFO reports be debunked to prevent hysteria and clogging of intelligence channels with UFO reports. An educational program would reduce "the current gullibility of the public and consequently their [sic] susceptibility to clever hostile propaganda"—that is, Soviet use of such reports for disinformation purposes.

Following the panel's recommendations, Blue Book, no longer under Ruppelt's direction, reverted to the Grudge practice of debunking after perfunctory investigation and continued this policy until it was closed down on December 17, 1969. To the American public it looked as if the U.S. government was out of the UFO business forever.

* * *

If one follows the public history of the official projects, a clear picture emerges of an Air Force strangely unconcerned (except for brief periods, specifically the Sign and early Blue Book eras) with some extraordinarily evidential reports—among them eyewitness and instrumented sightings of structured craftlike objects whose appearance and maneuvers clearly implied the operations of an advanced technology—which one would have thought had all kinds of national security implications.

Over the years civilian investigators would regularly hear reports of UFO encounters by military personnel who were warned not to discuss what they had seen and whose evidence (gun-camera film, for instance) was confiscated. Donald Keyhoe, a retired Marine Corps major and aviation journalist, became convinced as early as 1949 that a cover-up of a very big secret was in effect and argued as much in widely read books and magazine articles. He went on to direct a Washington-based lobbying organization, the National Investigations Committee on Aerial Phenomena

(NICAP), which sought Congressional hearings of the Air Force's handling of UFO reports. Keyhoe came to believe that the cover-up was being directed by a highly classified group of top scientists and government officials.

Others doubted that any such cover-up existed. Northwestern University astronomer J. Allen Hynek, who served for two decades as the Air Force's chief scientific consultant, thought Blue Book had "fouled up," as he put it, rather than covered up. Eventually he became disenchanted with what he saw as the project's chronic incompetence and sharply criticized it in his *The UFO Experience*. The standard academic history of the subject, David M. Jacobs' *The UFO Controversy in America*, agrees with Hynek's assessment.

But when the Bolender memo came to light, it was seen as confirmation of some ufologists' longheld suspicion that Blue Book was little more than a public-relations exercise and the really sensitive, evidential cases were going elsewhere. In Bolender's words, "reports…which could affect national security…are not part of the Blue Book system." But what were "the standard Air Force procedures" for handling these sensitive reports?

If the Roswell object was a UFO, the true history of our government's investigation of the UFO phenomenon was hidden from public view from the very beginning. In 1983, after the mass of evidence attesting to the reality of a crashed and recovered craft in July 1947 had convinced him of the reality of a cover-up, Bruce Maccabee of the Fund for UFO Research considered what this hidden history may have been. (Dr. Maccabee, a physicist employed by the Naval Surface Weapons Laboratory, has had considerable professional experience with classification procedures.) In a remarkable paper titled "Revised UFO History" he wrote:

> The Revised History proceeds from the assumption…that the Air Force knew by the middle of July 1947 that saucers were real and not manmade. Furthermore, it is not unreasonable to add the corollary that the Air Force knew that the technology represented by the [recovered] disc…was so far beyond our own that it could not be understood imme-

diately. Instead, it could take years of research in advanced physics to understand how a disc worked. Moreover, clearly whoever has discs "wins" in a military sense. Therefore it would become necessary to treat the disc as a military secret. This would mean containing all information about it within some small group. The military agencies best equipped for containing information are the intelligence agencies. Therefore the disc would be placed in the custody of an intelligence arm of the Air Force.

In Maccabee's view the public Air Force projects received "civilian/ military verbal reports while the top Air Force generals maintain[ed] absolute secrecy about the real thing. That way they got to collect data which might have been useful without having to reveal what they knew. To the outside world it looked as if the Air Force was fulfilling its duty to investigate unknowns in the sky but with little hope of finding anything."

The cover-up was directed by a small secret group of intelligence specialists who reported directly to the President, the Secretary of Defense, and the Joint Chiefs of Staff. Just below this group was another, larger one whose function was research, analysis, and field investigation. The Air Materiel Command, the Air Technical Intelligence Center, and the various public UFO projects at the bottom of this chain of command knew little or nothing of the secret work being done elsewhere, although each of these branches had at least one "mole" in its ranks. The mole's function was to be sure that the secret group learned immediately if—accidentally or otherwise—the public project got a sensitive case (such as a crash report) which was none of its business.

Maccabee believes that a principal purpose of the Air Force's relentless debunking of the subject was to discourage scientists from examining UFO data. A concerted effort by the scientific community to explain the UFO phenomenon, the engineers of the cover-up feared, might uncover the truth about extraterrestrial visitation and so blow the Ultimate Secret.

If Maccabee is right, it worked. Nonofficial UFO research was left in the hands of civilian ufologists lacking the technical expertise, funding, or institutional support to do what needed to be done. And scientists fell victim to a sophisticated hoax.

* * *

Let's call him Raymond Enright. That's not his name but this is his story:

Before 1972 Enright, a wealthy filmmaker and a prominent figure in the Republican Party of Southern California, had never given much thought to UFOs. To the extent that the subject had crossed his mind, he knew that the Air Force had investigated the reports and decided there was nothing to them.

Then one day in 1972 Enright was approached by Air Force officers who asked him if he would be interested in doing a feature on a secret project. Enright said he would be willing to consider it and was taken to a base and into a room. There he sat and listened as an officer described various classified projects, none especially interesting, which for one reason or another the Air Force felt it was ready to tell the American people about. In the course of the presentation the officer, in bland tones, began discussing the Air Force's UFO project, producing remarkable photographs and documents and talking about extraterrestrial visitors.

Enright was astonished. He said that he was under the impression the Air Force was no longer interested in UFOs. The officer said that was not true. In fact, the Air Force was deeply interested and had decided that at last it was ready to tell what it knew. Would Enright be interested in making a documentary film which would relate the UFO story to the public? He certainly would.

Over the next few months Enright had some amazing experiences. At one point he was taken to the Pentagon, where he met with two high-ranking Air Force officers who headed Blue Book in its last days. Publicly, both had been scathingly derisive of UFOs. Now, in an office in the Pentagon, they were showing Enright pictures not only of UFOs but of gray-skinned alien beings living and dead. Enright learned that between 1949 and 1952 an alien being who had survived a UFO crash lived in a "safe house" at Los Alamos, New Mexico. In 1952 he died of unknown causes. Enright saw pictures of him in the company of an Air Force officer who had been his constant companion during his brief life on earth.

Early in the course of his association with the Air Force officers, Enright was told that on April 26, 1964, a UFO landed by pre-arrangement at Holloman Air Force Base in New Mexico. Alien beings emerged from the craft and communicated with waiting scientists and military officers.

Enright was instructed to phone a certain officer at Holloman. This man would confirm the story and provide proof that it was true. Enright asked his producer to make the call and when he did, the officer said he didn't know what he was talking about. If he wanted to come to Holloman, he would get the standard tour that everybody else got.

Nonplussed, Enright phoned his principal contact (a former Blue Book officer) and was told that if he called Holloman personally in 20 minutes, he would get an entirely different response. Enright made the call and this time the officer promised full cooperation.

Enright went to Holloman and met the officer. He was given 800 feet of film of the Holloman landing and contact. He would be able to use this in his documentary.

He took the film back to his home in California. He did not copy it—later he explained that he felt he would have been acting in bad faith had he done so—and so did not have a record of it when subsequently he was directed to return it. The project was off. There were political problems. The Watergate scandal had Washington paralyzed, he was told, and it just wasn't the time to drop a big story like this on the American people. But yes, he should go ahead with the documentary. He could tell about the Holloman landing but he should describe it as "hypothetical."

He was given a list of psychologists whom he should ask what the public response to an official announcement of extraterrestrial visitation would be. The psychologists already knew the whole story but they wouldn't let on when they spoke on the record, to tell him they were sure the American people could handle such an announcement.

Enright made his documentary. It was a good, professional product, of the kind one would expect from a man of his professional background, but it was nothing exceptional, not what it could have been. It didn't change the world.

* * *

This is Linda Howe's story:

Howe is an independent film and television producer specializing in science, environmental issues, and international health. In the 1970s, as director of special projects for the Denver CBS-TV affiliate, she produced 12 documentaries. The one that attracted far and away the most attention was *Strange Harvest*, dealing with the then-widespread reports that cattle in Western and Midwestern states were being killed and mutilated by persons or forces unknown. Veterinary pathologists said the animals were dying of natural causes. Farmers, ranchers, and some lawmen thought the deaths were mysterious. Some even speculated that extraterrestrials were responsible.

In the fall of 1982, as Howe was working on a new documentary on an unrelated matter, she got a call from Home Box Office. The caller said the HBO people had been impressed with *Strange Harvest* and wanted to know if she would do a film on UFOs. In March 1983 she signed a contract with HBO for a feature to be titled *UFOs—The ET Factor*.

While in New York City to conduct business with the HBO people, she had dinner with Peter Gersten, a lawyer who had battled the government to force it to release UFO documents, and science writer Patrick Huyghe. Gersten had some material from a certain Air Force officer—we'll call him Major Cody—in a sensitive position at a certain base in a Western state. Cody had told Gersten he would be willing to talk about an alleged UFO landing at another Air Force base. At Howe's behest Gersten called Cody and a meeting was arranged.

On April 9 Howe met Cody in an office on the base. As it turned out, Cody had little to say about the landing. He wanted to talk about something else.

He asked Howe to move from the chair on which she was sitting to another in the middle of the room. Howe guessed later that this was to facilitate the surreptitious recording of their conversation.

"My superiors have asked me to show you this," Cody said. He handed her a document several pages long and told her she could not copy it, nor could she take notes. All she could do was read it in his presence and ask some questions.

The document, a photocopy on plain white paper, gave no indication anywhere which government, military, or scientific agency (if any) had prepared the report, titled "A Briefing Paper for the President of the United States of America on the Subject of Unidentified Flying Vehicles." The title did not specify which President it had in mind, nor did the document list a date (so far as Howe recalls today) which would have linked it to a particular administration.

The first paragraph, written—as was everything that followed—in what Howe characterizes as "dry bureaucratese," listed dates and locations of crashes and retrievals of UFOs and their occupants. The latter were invariably described as 3-1/2 to four feet tall, gray-skinned and hairless, with oversized heads, large eyes, and no noses. It was now known, the document stated on a subsequent page, that these beings, from a nearby solar system, have been here for many thousands of years. Through genetic manipulation they influenced the course of human evolution and in a sense created us. They had also helped shape our religious beliefs.

The July 1947 crash at Roswell was mentioned; so, however, was another at Roswell, in 1949. This time one of the occupants survived the wreck and he was taken to a safe house at Los Alamos. He was befriended, if that was the word, by an Air Force officer who became his constant companion until the creature died of unknown causes on June 18, 1952. The being was named "EBE," for Extraterrestrial Biological Entity. Subsequently he would be called EBE-1, since in later years another such being, EBE-2, would take up residence in a safe house. After that a third, EBE-3, appeared on the scene and was now living in secret at an American base.

Cody talked about a landing at Holloman AFB on the morning of April 25, 1964—12 hours after the famous Socorro, New Mexico, landing of around six o'clock the evening before. Military and scientific personnel at the base knew it was coming—electronic communication with the alien occupants of the vehicle had been established sometime earlier—and so they were ready with five cameras. The film, taken from both air and ground, showed three aliens—EBEs emerging from the craft, one in front, two behind.

Cody said Howe would be given 68,000 feet of film of the Holloman landing and also of the late EBE-1 and these were to be used in her documentary, which would tell the story of how U.S. officials learned that the earth is being visited and what they have done about it. Cody mentioned Enright, saying there had been an effort to effect a release of this information a decade earlier, but the political conditions hadn't been right.

On the last page the document cited the various official UFO projects. Blue Book was among them but the document indicated it had existed solely to take heat off the Air Force and to draw attention from the real projects, such as Sigma (the on-going electronic communications effort), Snow Bird (research and development from the study of an intact spacecraft left by the aliens as a gift), and Aquarius (the umbrella operation under which the research and contact efforts were coordinated). The document also mentioned a now-defunct Project Garnet. Garnet's purpose was to investigate extraterrestrial influence on human evolution. After "all questions about human evolution" were answered, the document stated, the project closed down.

Cody told Howe of another group, something called "MJ-12." "MJ," he said, stood for "Majority."* It was a policy-making body whose membership consisted of 12 very high-ranking government scientists, military officers, and intelligence officials. These were the men who made the decisions governing the cover-up and the contacts.

The meeting lasted, Howe recalls, about three hours. Cody told her that he and his "superiors" would stay in touch with her.

Over the next weeks Howe had a number of phone conversations with Cody, mostly about technical problems related to converting old film to use on modern film. She also spoke on several occasions with three other men, two of whom would call her on the phone but whom she never met personally. She met the third in Washington months later.

Cody suggested that eventually she might be allowed to film an interview with EBE-3. But the current film project was to have a historical emphasis; it would deal with events between 1949 and 1964. If at some point she did meet EBE3, however, there was no way she could prepare herself for the "shock and fear" of meeting an alien being.

Howe had informed the HBO people of all this and she urged them to prepare themselves, legally and otherwise, for the repercussions that would surely follow the release of the film. The HBO people told her she would have to secure a letter of intent from the U.S. government with a legally-binding commitment to release the 68,000 feet of film. When Howe called Cody about it, he said, "I'll work on it." He said he would mail the letter directly to HBO.

Howe flew to New York. HBO told her it would not authorize funds for the film production until all the evidence was in hand and it was examined in the company of the Secretaries of State and Defense and the Joint Chiefs of Staff. But proceed anyway, they told her. Howe was furious at both HBO and Cody.

She called Cody at the base. "I have good news and bad news," he told her. She and a small crew would soon be able to interview the retired colonel (then a captain) who had spent three years with EBE-I. The bad news was that it would be three months before the 68,000 feet of film of EBE-I and the Holloman landing/contact would be available. Meanwhile, in order to screen the material Howe would have to sign three security oaths and undergo a security check.

In June, Cody called to say he was officially out of the project. From now on she would be dealing with others. To Howe this was a blow because Cody was the only one she could call. She did not know how to get in touch with the others and always had to wait for them to contact her.

By October the contacts had decreased significantly. That same month her contract with HBO expired. Later that year she was directed to meet one of the contacts in Washington. He showed her a badge which identified him as a member of a certain government agency. His words were to this effect: We know it's difficult. We would like your help. We're trying to find a way to go forward with this but political conditions are awkward. We must have this film on television no later than 1986. He did not explain what this last statement meant.

In the end it all came to nothing. Today Howe looks back and says, "I don't know what the real truth is but I think I saw glimpses of it. This story is much bigger than I ever expected. But I saw it in a hall of mirrors, with quicksand as a floor."

* * *

This is Bill Moore and Jaime Shandera's story:

In early September 1980 Moore, coauthor with Charles Berlitz of *The Roswell Incident*, was on his way to Washington, D.C., from his home in Arizona to attend a debate on UFOs scheduled at the Smithsonian Institution. Along the way he was promoting his recently-published book in radio and television interviews. He was also continuing the investigation that had consumed him since 1978, when he and Stanton Friedman suspected that the Roswell case might be the one crashed-saucer story that could be documented.

He had done a radio show in Omaha and was in the station lobby, suitcase in hand, on his way to catch a plane which was to leave within the hour when a receptionist sitting at a desk in the lobby asked if he was Mr. Moore.

He had a phone call.

Moore picked up the phone and heard the voice of a man who identified himself as a colonel at nearby Offutt Air Force Base. He said, "We think you're the only one we've heard who seems to know what he's talking about." He asked if he and Moore could get together and discuss things further. Moore apologized, saying that wasn't possible because he was leaving town in a few minutes. He took down the man's phone number and thought no more about it.

He went on to Washington. On September 8, on his way back home, he did a radio show in Albuquerque. On the way out of the studio the receptionist told him he had a phone call. The caller, who identified himself as an officer from nearby Kirtland AFB, said, "We think you're the only one we've heard about who seems to know what he's talking about."

Moore said, "Where have I heard that before?"

They agreed to meet at a restaurant in the area. The caller said he would be wearing a red tie. And that was how it all began.

Almost two years later, in May 1982, Moore approached someone he knew, a veteran film and television producer he'd worked with on a UFO movie that hadn't panned out. Jaime Shandera, Moore knew, was a level-headed guy who had no real background in ufology and no firm opinions one way or another. Moore needed someone who could look at things objectively. He had lived with it too long already and was exhausted. Besides that, his sources wanted to tell the story on film and the only filmmaker Moore knew was Shandera.

So Moore related the whole story to Shandera, who agreed it was awfully interesting. He did not, however, care to go to the considerable trouble of raising money for the film himself. He suggested a friend, a CBS producer who had recently moved to Los Angeles from New York.

Shandera talked with the producer, who said that if anybody but Shandera had told him such a tale he would have shown him the door. But the producer was hiring an investigator and maybe he could look into this.

Shandera had met Moore's principal source at the Air Force base where he was stationed. He was impressed. The guy was personable and straightforward. He said he was fronting for a group, including some powerful people, who wanted the cover-up ended. There were other powerful people who were opposed to their efforts, he said.

Shandera decided he wanted in. Moore had been at the beck and call of these people—ten of them in all, six active, four periodically active (they'd show up for six months or so, then never be heard from again). Mostly they called on the phone but Moore had met some of them on a number of occasions. Sometimes he could contact them. They'd give him a phone number which would be good for a while; then one day he'd call and there'd be nothing.

It looked like a big, big story and Shandera believed in it enough to quit his job and devote full time to it. His wife, also a television producer, paid the bills while Shandera chased the Ultimate Secret. That was the way it had to be. You had to play it exactly their way or they'd drop you.

It turned out to be years of cloak-and-dagger stuff. Phone calls directing you to some distant city, where a stranger would appear and tell you something or hand you something—such as CIA documents about EBE-3—and vanish back into the crowd. One time Moore flew from airport to airport, getting directions at each stop from a voice on a pay phone. Eventually he ended up in a certain motel in upstate New York. He was to eat at the restaurant across the street—the caller even recommended a particular item on the menu—and to sit by the window. By 5:00 p.m. he was to be back at his motel room.

At precisely 5:00 p.m. someone knocked on the door and a man appeared with a bundle under his arm. He said to Moore that he had 17 minutes to do whatever he wanted with what he was about to be given. He could copy it but he couldn't keep it. Moore had a camera with him and did his best. The document purported to be a briefing paper telling newly-elected President Jimmy Carter about MJ-12, Project Aquarius, the little gray men and all the rest.

Moore learned later that the individual responsible for seeing to it that he got the document got into trouble: All Moore knew for sure was that not long afterwards two FBI agents called on him. They were friendly but they wanted to know about his loyalty and motives. UFOs were discussed.

The sources spoke of two UFO crashes, the 1947 one at Roswell, another along the Texas-Mexico border in December 1950. A humanoid was found alive in 1949 and housed at Los Alamos between 1949 and 1953, when he died of unknown causes. An Air Force captain, now a retired colonel, had been his constant companion during those years and much was learned from EBE-I, who was the "mechanic" on the craft that had gone down. Moore and Shandera were not told where this crash occurred; they know only of the two in 1947 and 1950.

In response to the Roswell incident MJ-12—the MJ stands for "Majestic"—was set up by executive order of President Truman on September 24, 1947, and its first head was Vannevar Bush, the President's chief science adviser. The current head of MJ-12 is Vice President and former CIA Director George Bush. Project Aquarius is an umbrella group in which all the various compartments dealing with ET-related issues perform their various functions. Project Sigma conducts electronic communication with the extraterrestrials, part of an on-going contact project run through the National Security Agency since 1964, beginning with the Holloman incident of April 26.

President Reagan knows all this. In fact, it fascinates him to the degree that, in one source's words, he "eats it up like candy." He hints at it in public speeches and private conversations (including one with Soviet Premier Gorbachev during the Reykjavik summit) where he cautions that one day the human race may have to unite in the face of hostile extraterrestrials.

The source to whom Moore and Shandera would feel personally

most close was an Air Force intelligence officer they call "Falcon." (They have given all their informants the names of birds.) When Falcon calls Moore, he always starts out by asking about his family. Moore has met him over 100 times and now knows Falcon's family. Shandera knows him well too.

I have seen and heard Falcon myself, but I don't know what he looks like or what his voice sounds like. I saw him on a videotape (said to have been made in February 1987) in Shandera's living room in North Hollywood on November 4, 1987. Falcon's face is in shadow, his voice electronically altered. He is sitting in a motel room and a reporter—the CBS producer's investigator—is asking him questions. The producer is filming.

Falcon is describing the nature and the subject of the cover-up. What is being covered up, he says, is visitation by nine different extraterrestrial races. He says nothing more about seven of them and only briefly mentions another, this one made up of aliens five feet tall, slender, with hair and slanting eyes. Mostly he talks about the little gray-skinned people who come from the third planet surrounding Zeta Reticuli. They have been here for 25,000 years and influenced the direction of human evolution. They have also played a large role in the shaping of our religious beliefs.

He talks about Majestic-12 and Project Aquarius. He says he doesn't know who the current members of MJ-12 are. He does say, however, that John Poindexter, Harold Brown, and James Scheslinger are among those in the know. He talks about how four groups, each consisting of 200 persons, conduct secret UFO investigations in four assigned areas of the United States. He mentions the Roswell and Texas-Mexico crash. He says the bodies of the occupants, when autopsied, proved to be remarkably uncomplicated, with relatively few internal organs.

He says it first proved difficult to communicate with EBE-I. Eventually a speech device was implanted in his throat and he was able to speak in an English that was usually although not always understanable.

Falcon claims that some people within the cover-up want it to end. The American people are being prepared for the reality of alien visitation through the vehicle of popular entertainment. He mentions the Steven Spielberg movies *Close Encounters of the Third Kind* (its climax a thinly fictionalized version of the Holloman landing) and *ET*.

He says that at CIA headquarters in Langley, Virginia, there is a thick book which is referred to as "The Bible." The Bible contains all the various project reports on aspects of alien visitation. Falcon has read some of it.

* * *

Who are these people? And why are they saying these things?

Moore and Shandera have met them on military bases often enough to know they are who they say they are. If there were any doubts on that score, they ended when Moore received a phone call from a source who told him that a Korean airliner had been shot down over the Soviet Union—before the story hit the press. They do not think they are the victims of a sophisticated disinformation scheme, but they don't know this for sure. They think the contacts are officially sanctioned.

They also know, from long experience, that the sources talk a better game than they play. Moore and Shandera have been promised a "truckload" of documents but so far have been given less than a glove compartment's worth. One of these, the famous (or notorious) MJ-12 briefing paper for President-elect Eisenhower, arrived in a plain brown wrapper at Shandera's residence in December 1984 and later, following cryptically written guidance on two separate postcards, each manufactured in Ethiopia, each mailed from New Zealand, he and Moore found in the National Archives a memo from Eisenhower's assistant Gen. Robert Cutler to Gen. Nathan Twining referring to an "MJ-12 SSP [Special Studies Project] briefing" to "take place during the already scheduled White House meeting of July 16…"

Although "MJ-12" is not referred to as a UFO project—a curious omission if the memo is a hoax—critics have charged that it was planted. Some have hinted darkly that Moore and Shandera planted it in the Archives themselves after forging the MJ-12 document. This is unlikely for a number of reasons. (It should be noted that the MJ-12 document did not come to light until May 31, 1987, when it was reported on the front page of the *London Observer*, and then the person releasing it was British writer Timothy Good, who secured a copy through entirely independent sources rumored to be connected with the Ministry of Defense.) Moore and his associate Stanton Friedman have effectively refuted debunkers' sometimes poorly-thought-out charges against the document.

Yet the MJ-12 document is hardly good evidence of anything and skepticism in the absence of firm validation is a rational response. The issue will be resolved not by ufologists or professional debunkers but by document examiners.

After 7-1/2 years for Moore and 5-1/2 for Shandera, the two are tired and want to resume normal lives, including jobs that, unlike Ultimate Secret-chasing, pay salaries. They tell their sources that they are about to release what they have—a story of some strange encounters with agents of the U.S. government, a videotape, a few more documents which are bound to be as furiously disputed as the ones they have already released—and the sources say fine, if you want to, go ahead; but if you don't, we'll have some very interesting stuff for you.

This past October their sources told them to collect some expensive camera equipment and fly to Washington, where they would be met by someone who would take them to a certain place in a wooded area. There they would be permitted to interview and film EBE-3.

When they arrived in Washington, no one was waiting.

If, in the curious and confused case of crashed discs, cover-ups, little gray men, MJ-12, and Project Aquarius, it is safe to say one thing, it is this: The hunt will continue and the prey will remain elusive.

Beyond the Known
John Keel
March 1990

The Fugo Balloons

It was not known to the general public that during the war the Japanese were attempting to use fire balloons against the West Coast of the United States.—*Manhattan Project: The Untold Story of the Making of the Atomic Bomb* by Stephane Groueff, 1967.

WHILE AMERICAN SCHOOLCHILDREN were engaged in scrap metal drives for the war effort in the 1940s, Japanese children were put to work on a much more imaginative project. They were asked to build large paper balloons that could be filled with hydrogen and set adrift in the jet stream. Ultimately, a total of 9,000 of these *Fugo* balloons were built and launched. How many finally reached the U.S. will never be known, but we do know that several did manage to make the long trip. (Incidentally, many years later it was revealed that the American scrap metal drives were a phony and that the scrap metal collected was never used. The whole thing was just a scheme to give schoolchildren a sense of participation in the war.) Wartime Japan was faced with many critical shortages. The balloons were a practical idea because they could be made of readily-available brown rice paper. Artistic Japanese children decorated the paper panels with fierce dragons, snow-topped mountains, flowers, and anti-American slogans. The panels were carefully glued together and reinforced with silken strings. An indestructible mylar-like material was used for "sails" on some balloons, with spars fashioned of a lightweight pressed-rice kind of plastic. This pseudo-plastic was widely used in Japan during the war years because wood was virtually unobtainable. It was fireproof and wouldn't melt (unlike the early plastics used in the West, such as forms of bakelite).

Each balloon was equipped with a clever altimeter and system of weights. Whenever the balloon dipped below a certain altitude, the altimeter would trigger a release that would drop a weight. When all the weights were gone and the balloon still sank to a low altitude, the altimeter would finally release the payload—an incendiary bomb. The balloons were 33 feet in diameter. As more and more of them were launched, they became more sophisticated. Eventually some of them were attached to tracking devices and gadgets designed to attract or confuse radar. Japanese submarines spread across the Pacific and tried to check their westward journey in an effort to ascertain if the scheme was really working.

One ingenious attachment was a simple sphere made of aluminum. It was lightweight and dangled beneath the balloon until the altimeter finally released it. When a radar beam struck the sphere, the signal would ricochet in such a way that when it returned to the radar transmitter it would produce a huge image on the tracking screen. It looked as if the radar had detected an object 700–1,000 feet in diameter! The Japanese subs would know they had picked up one of their balloons, but U.S. Naval ships were totally baffled by the gigantic—and impossible—returns. After the war, the

U.S. Navy even released some of their reports about these huge radar "ghosts" of the Pacific. And for many years after WW II, the spheres were found in many odd places from Australia to the Himalaya Mountains, probably dropped by Fugo balloons that had wandered way off course.

Another anti-radar technique, developed by the British early in the war, was called "chaff" by Allied pilots. The Germans and Japanese were soon using this, too. At first it consisted of chopped-up tinfoil that was dumped out of planes and caused "snow" on enemy radar screens. Later, tiny strips of aluminum foil were used. These strips were cut to the wave lengths of the radar transmitters. Some were only a few centimeters long while others, called "rope," were several feet in length. Some balloons had pieces of this stuff of varying lengths dangling from their payload. When picked up by radar, they produced a scrambled image that suggested a flight of birds. Other balloons were constructed to dump batches of "chaff" at periodic intervals along their flight path.

Imagine how weird some of these balloons must have looked, with silvery streamers dangling from them and wide vanes spread out to act as sails and help speed them across the Pacific. Those that managed to reach the U.S. were undoubtedly seen by thousands of people, though no one would ever suspect that they came from hostile Japan 5,000 miles away.

An Incredible Coincidence

America's top secret during the war years was the Manhattan Project to build the atomic bomb. One of the super-secret plutonium processing plants was located in a barren area called Hanford in the state of Washington.

"One day a mysterious power failure occurred somewhere in the current, immediately triggering the safety controls of the reactors," according to Groueff's *Manhattan Project*. "What had happened? Was it sabotage? Colonel Matthias' security men swarmed into the area and imposed the strictest secrecy on all information concerning the power failure. Only the top Du Pont people were informed confidentially about the cause of the trouble: a Japanese balloon."

It does seem unreal, you must admit, that a flimsy paper balloon could cross the vast Pacific on an uncontrolled flight and then effectively settle on the power lines leading to one of America's most secret—and isolated—installations. But it happened. More than once!

"At least two Japanese balloons fell in the Hanford area," Groueff states, "and one of them dropped on the power line between Bonneville and Grand Coulee, thus interrupting electric current and thereby triggering the safety mechanism of the reactors."

Only the very highest officials in the government knew that America was under siege. We now know that at least one forest fire in Canada was started by a Fugo balloon and four campers in Montana were killed by one. The latter incident set off the government censors.

"The first two balloons to be seen in the United States fell in Montana and North Dakota and were reported in the Japanese press a week later," Groueff wrote. "Since only local American newspapers had mentioned the incidents, Japanese spies were obviously reading the smallest country publications. After that any mention of the balloons in American papers was censored out."

Post-War Censorship

Fugo balloons must have been a great embarrassment to American military authorities. They eluded our radar and we had no way to combat those paper balloons constructed by schoolchildren. In typical bureaucratic fashion, our leaders had to ignore their existence and the public remained ignorant of the menace, even long after the war ended.

"On January 4, 1945, the Office of Censorship asked newspaper editors and radio broadcasters to give no publicity whatsoever to balloon incidents. This voluntary censorship was adhered to from coast to coast, a remarkable self-restraint in a free-press-conscious country…" (*Japan's World War II Balloon Bomb Attacks on North America,* Smithsonian Institution, 1973.)

A propaganda office, the Office of War Information (O.W.I.), had been set up in Washington during WW II. The Office of Censorship, a branch of O.W.I., was primarily concerned with keeping the Manhattan Project secret. Their methodology was simple enough. They would send letters to the editors of the 2,000-plus newspapers in the country asking them to avoid certain subjects. It worked.

"In a 'strictly confidential' note to editors and broadcasters, the Office of Censorship stated: 'Cooperation from the press and radio under this request has been excellent despite the fact that Japanese free balloons are reaching the United States, Canada, and Mexico in increasing numbers... There is no question that your refusal to broadcast information about these balloons has baffled the Japanese, annoyed and hindered them, and has been an important contribution to security." (Article, "Jap Balloons Dropped Bombs on U.S. During World War II" by R. C. Mikesh, *National Enquirer*, July 28, 1968.)

So we know the balloons were accidentally bombing Mexico and Canada, too. Thanks to the self-imposed censorship, we will never know just how many of the balloons reached this continent or what the total damage really was.

Still More Secrecy

Japan, somewhat unnerved by our atomic bombs, surrendered in August 1945. The war ended, our boys came home, the Office of Censorship was disbanded, and the launching of Fugo balloons ceased. But something strange happened. Fugo balloons continued to appear over the United States for years!

Every Fortean has heard the strange reports of old newspapers suddenly fluttering out of a clear sky, giving no clue as to where they had been in the months or years since they were published. Lightweight items may float around in the atmosphere for 100 years before dropping into your backyard.

Of the 9,000 balloons sent aloft by the Japanese, it is safe to assume that most of them finally landed harmlessly in the ocean. A few reached North America, and the rest got caught in the peculiar winds and eddies of the upper stratosphere where all those old newspapers, hats, frogs, and blocks of ice drift about. Then, from time to time, one would crash to earth and thoroughly mystify all those who had never heard about the secret balloon invasion.

Almost a year after the war, one turned up on the border of Colorado and New Mexico, according to the *Durango Chapbook,* July 1946. "On April 19, 1946, two men excitedly reported that Navajo Lake had been bombed by a flying brown thing. They said a silvery object had been dropped from a brown sphere. Just before it reached the water it exploded and showered flames in all directions. The sphere soared away."

The jet stream seemed to carry many of the balloons on a curved course from Oregon to New Mexico. In early 1947, they were still drifting down. Reports were scanty, but elements of the U.S. Army were clearly interested.

"Two big, brown paper balloons, one of which had Christmas tree 'icicles' hanging from it, were found by campers near Malheur Lake this Spring," a brief item in *The West Oregonian* revealed on September 27, 1947. "The remnants of a third, with a strange metal instrument attached, were found in Klamath County in August. Army personnel visited the site and removed all the debris. All three balloons appeared to be handmade, according to witnesses, and contained mysterious Oriental-like inscriptions."

A curtain of secrecy continued to shield the unwary public from the explosive balloons in their midst. The biggest breech of this security occurred in July 1947, at the height of the first "flying saucer scare" when, after a severe storm, the remains of one of the balloons was found on a ranch in Lincoln County, New Mexico. Local newspapers described the find, and the wire services picked up the story. Later, military authorities carted away the materials and announced it was nothing but a "weather balloon." Obviously, they were determined to keep the existence of the Fugo balloons a secret two years after the war. In fact, few knew about the Fugo project until the 1950s, when a small Japanese booklet on the subject was published.

There is evidence that the balloons were still bombing New Mexico in 1949, four years after the end of hostilities. In his 1953 book, *Flying Saucers From Outer Space,* Donald Keyhoe describes the "Red Spray saucers" which appeared near Albuquerque, dropped to about 200 feet, exploded, and sprayed fire in all directions.

There was a mysterious explosion of an incendiary-type device over a Brazilian beach in 1957. It scattered pieces of magnesium, a prime ingredient for WW II incendiary bombs, and is still considered a "crashed saucer" by UFO cultists. It does seem unlikely that a bomb launched in 1945 would turn up in Brazil 12 years later, but it is possible.

Roswell Revisited

Military secrecy worked so well that the Fugo project would have been completely forgotten if a couple of the damnable things had not knocked out the lights at Hanford and thus found immortality in the literature on the development of the atomic bomb. When the U.S. Government Printing Office published the Smithsonian's report on the subject in 1973, only a few random aviation historians paid any attention to it.

A 1950 bestseller, *Behind the Flying Saucers* by *Variety* columnist Frank Scully, embellished the New Mexico incidents with complicated tales of dead "little men," the autopsies of same, and other fanciful rumors. Although thoroughly disproven later, Scully's stories became an integral part of the burgeoning flying saucer lore known as the "Roswell Incident."

Horror novelist Whitley Strieber visited Roswell in the 1980s and tracked down some of the surviving witnesses. In the Afterword to *Majestic*, he repeats the testimony of some of the witnesses:

"Marcel went on to describe what he had found. 'There was all kinds of stuff—small beams about three-eighths or a half-inch square with some sort of hieroglyphics on them that nobody could decipher. These looked something like balsa wood, and were of about the same weight, except they were not wood at all. They were very hard, although flexible, and would not burn. There was a great deal of unusual parchment-like substance which was brown in color and extremely strong, and a great number of small pieces of a metal like tinfoil, except that it wasn't tinfoil.' Later 'Mac' Brazel's daughter Bessie described the paper as having apparent flowers pressed in it."

Unfortunately, Strieber did not have the last word. Several books and countless magazine articles have been inspired by the "Roswell Incident," and several more are due to appear in 1990–91. The Fugo balloons will be with us for a long time.

UFO Reporter
Jerome Clark
June 1990

The Mystery of S-4

For the past two years or so, Don Schmitt and Kevin D. Randle of the J. Allen Hynek Center for UFO Studies have been engaged in a reinvestigation of the Roswell incident, the reported crash of a UFO in Lincoln County, New Mexico, in July 1947. As of February of this year, they had interviewed over 170 persons directly or indirectly involved with the event, which is emerging as perhaps the central event in the early history of the UFO phenomenon. From it there followed, it appears, the greatest cover-up of the century. Schmitt and Randle's book on the case (titled simply *Roswell*) will be published late this year.

For most of UFO history, stories of crashed discs were rejected by serious ufologists, me among them, for one good reason: there was no evidence to support them. Although crash tales had circulated since the late 1940s—in other words from the beginning of the UFO age—some (most notoriously the Aztec, New Mexico, crash hoax chronicled in Frank Scully's 1950 bestseller *Behind the Flying Saucers*) were exposed as fraudulent. Others were "friend-of-a-friend" types of yarns (known to folklorists as "foaftales"). A minority involved alleged first-person testimony, but even when the informants seemed sincere (not always the case), there was no way to verify so fantastic an assertion. Investigators need more than one source for stories of this kind.

All this changed in the late 1970s when William L. Moore and Stanton T. Friedman focused on one case which seemed investigatable. In 1980 Moore, with Charles Berlitz, wrote a not-very-good book based on the preliminary investigation, *The Roswell Incident.* Fortunately, Moore and Friedman continued their investigation over the next years and by 1985 were presenting a solid case to the UFO community. Schmitt and Randle's further work has considerably strengthened that case. Yet the appearance in ufology of a credible, powerfully documented crash/retrieval case did not end the rumors, speculations, foaftales and outright hoaxes about these matters. Some of the yarns had official sponsorship (see my last three articles in this column). Others may have had some factual basis but had no independent confirmation. Others represented human beings' innate (and essentially innocent) need to invent and spread tales for no other reason than they are wondrous or scary. Some were out-and-out fiction, invented by con artists seeking to extract money from gullible souls.

After Roswell

Much of the current speculation, folklore, fantasy, and conspiracy theorizing centers on the question of what happened after the Roswell incident. Little of it has the informed good sense of physicist Bruce Maccabee's 1983 paper *Revised UFO History,* a well-reasoned piece, by a man professionally familiar with classification procedures, on how official agencies would have handled the Roswell material. Except for its premise (that the government possesses the remains of an extraterrestrial vehicle), Maccabee's treatment is unsensational and matter-of-fact. His is probably the only such speculation that does not insult one's intelligence. The problem is that very little direct evidence of the hidden history has surfaced. So far we can see clearly only where it began, on the Mac Brazel ranch in New Mexico, but we have practically no idea where it went from there.

MJ-12

A disputed document, almost certainly a forgery, purports to be a briefing paper prepared by a supersecret organization called "Majestic-12," consisting of top government scientists and military officers who oversaw research on wreckage and bodies from the Roswell incident and another crash in 1950. Logic tells us that, if UFO spacecraft have crashed and been kept secret all this time, some such project, whether designated MJ-12 or something else, was certain to have been put into operation. One of the principal concerns, of course, would be to unlock the secrets of extraterrestrial technology.

The Mystery of Area 51

On November 11 and 13, 1989, KLAS-TV, the ABC affiliate in Las Vegas, Nevada, carried an astonishing story on its evening news show, the result of a 1-1/2-year investigation by reporter George Knapp. The subject was one Robert Lazar, identified as a physicist who worked at a highly-classified government laboratory where the U.S. government is studying interplanetary hardware.

Lazar claimed to have been employed at Area 51, situated in a corner of the Nevada Test Site, a remote location ringed by the Groom Mountains and desert expanses. For several decades some of the most sensitive military and intelligence research and development have been going on there. The U-2 and SR-71 spy planes were tested at the site. Other projects which have emerged from Area 51 are the Stealth and Strategic Defense Initiative ("Star Wars") technology. For years rumors have circulated that some of the work going on there is literally out of this world. Much of the speculation has been sparked by persistent reports of unusual lights seen maneuvering over the area—lights that have flown at great speeds, then stopped suddenly and hovered before accelerating again, behaving, in other words, in ways that seem impossible for conventional aircraft.

As the story goes, Lazar was hired to work at Area 51 in a location designated S-4. The Navy wanted him to work on advanced propulsion systems, and Lazar was given classified technical papers to read. Their contents amazed him; they described propulsion systems far in advance of anything conventional physics could have conceived. "The power source is an antimatter reactor," he told Knapp. "They run gravity amplifiers. There is [sic] actually two parts to the drive mechanism. It's a bizarre technology. There is [sic] no physical hookups between any of the systems in there. They use gravity as a wave, using wave guides that look like microwaves."

The walls of the work areas displayed posters showing a disc ascending from the ground; the caption read, "They're here." In due course Lazar was taken into a hangar where he saw a disc. Although he was instructed to walk by the vehicle and not look directly at it, he touched it briefly as he passed it. Later he saw the object in flight and was also allowed to view eight other craft in connecting hangars separated by large bay doors. Each had a distinctive appearance but all were disc-shaped. One looked brand new, but another had a large hole in the bottom and a corresponding one at the top, leading him to speculate that a missile or anti-aircraft projectile had pierced it.

His superiors told him nothing about the nature of these craft or the circumstances of their recovery. Once, however, when he looked inside one, he saw "it had really small chairs," as if its pilots were of shorter-than-human stature. That caused things, he said, "to click together just all too fast." After observing the discs in the air, he was convinced that no terrestrial technology could have accomplished what he was seeing. But what clinched matters for him was his discovery that an element unknown to earthly science, element 115, played a major role in the development of the gravity-harnessing technology. Five hundred pounds of it is stored in lead casings. It would be, he said, "impossible to synthesize an element that heavy here on earth...The substance has to come from a place where super-heavy elements could have been produced naturally."

Not even the U.S. Congress knows about any of this, Lazar claimed. The funding probably was hidden within the Star Wars budget, he thought.

Tight Security through Fear

Security was maintained by keeping employees in a state of nearly constant fear. "They did everything but physically hurt me," he said. On more than one occasion a gun was put to his head as security personnel were "slamming their fingers into my chest, screaming into my ear." They would even come to his house from time to time to threaten both him and his wife.

Reporter Knapp interviewed Lazar's neighbor, a real-estate appraiser named Gene Huff, to whom Lazar had confided his story before going public with it. Huff said that over two consecutive weekends he, Lazar and several others had filmed a fast-moving, glowing object which rose up from the Groom Mountains and executed aerial acrobatics for a period of time. The resulting videotape was run in the course of Knapp's account.

Knapp said he had found others who knew about the extraordinary projects at S-4. It is, he said, "common knowledge among those with high-security clearances that recovered alien discs are stored at the Nevada Test Site," according to an individual whom Knapp identified as a "technician in a highly sensitive position." Claims of sightings of discs on the ground or in the air just above the site were made by a "Las Vegas professional who once served in the military and was stationed at the test site," by a "man who once worked at Groom Lake as a technician," and by an "airman who worked at [nearby] Nellis [AFB] at a radar installation."

Truth or ?

These are extraordinary claims. Readers should be warned that the truth of these claims is far from certain. Elements of ambiguity cloud the picture.

For one thing, as Knapp reported, "Checking out Lazar's credentials proved to be a difficult task." Lazar claimed to have degrees from the Massachusetts Institute of Technology, but MIT declared it had never heard of him. A purported association with the California Institute of Technology also failed to check out. And later, when physicist-ufologist Stanton T. Friedman looked into Lazar's background, he found that Lazar was not a member of the American Physical Society.

Yet other claims of Lazar's were verified, despite official denials. For example, he said he had worked with one of the world's largest particle-beam accelerators at the Los Alamos National Laboratories. When Los Alamos said this was not so, Knapp learned that it was "either mistaken or…lying." Lazar is listed in a 1982 Los Alamos lab phone book, and a news clipping from the same year mentions Lazar's employment at the laboratory. Lazar said, "They're trying to make me look nonexistent."

During his investigation, Knapp had Lazar undergo a series of polygraph examinations, with conflicting results. The first examiner gave him two tests; Lazar passed one and flunked the other. Another examiner gave him four tests and declared him truthful. A third examiner studied the charts of the previous tests and endorsed the second examiner's conclusions. A fourth disagreed, saying it appeared to him that Lazar was reporting something he had heard, not something he had witnessed directly. The second examiner opined that the ambiguities in the test results had to do not with the subject's dishonesty but with his acute anxiety about testifying to sensitive national-security, and possibly even life-threatening, matters. Knapp told his audience, "The polygraphers…decided they would not issue a final statement on truthfulness until more specific testing can be conducted. And that's where it stands."

Lazar also underwent hypnosis. The hypnotist, Layne Keck, was told only that Lazar wanted help in recalling the contents of papers, contents unspecified, he had seen. While hypnotized Lazar began speaking of pictures of "desks," or so Keck heard him saying; soon, though, he realized "it was discs that he was referring to. And at that moment I realized we were into something...pretty heavy." Keck, who often works with the police, concluded Lazar was telling the truth as he knew it.

The Work Goes On

Both journalists and ufologists are pursuing the investigation. One UFO investigator, Grant Cameron, tells me that so far the evidence suggests there is a "50-50 chance" the story is true. One point in Lazar's favor is that he has sought neither money nor additional publicity, and quite early in the game separated himself from individuals who tried to exploit him or get him to endorse their own cover-up fantasies. Knapp's own investigation, as reported on KLAS' evening news show, convinced him that Lazar is on the level. But the rest of us would be advised to be very, very cautious. One of life's lessons is that if something sounds too good to be true, there's a reason for it: it is.

The Roswell Furor

January 1991

IN HIS COLUMN, *Beyond the Known* (FATE, March 1990), John Keel proposed that the debris found at Roswell, in what is now known as the "Roswell Incident," came from a World War II Fugo balloon bomb from Japan. The result has set off a storm of controversy in the UFO world as well as a barrage of letters sent to FATE and Mr. Keel. Below are two responses to that column by some people who are important in the UFO community. Following each is the author's response. Opinions expressed are those of the respective writers.

A Letter from Stanton Friedman

As the scientist who began the investigation of the so-called Roswell incident more than a decade ago I am appalled at the grossly inaccurate and misleading presentation of it in John Keel's column on Fugo balloons in the March 1990 issue (FATE, *Beyond the Known*). There is a great amount of serious research that has been done and published which Keel apparently hasn't bothered to examine because of his own obvious anti-ETH [Extra-Terrestrial Hypothesis] bias. There is the 1980 book, *The Roswell Incident*, by Berlitz and Moore for which Moore and I did about 95 percent of the research including dealing with 60 persons connected with the case. Between us, he and I did six more papers culminating in his 49-page paper (1985) "Crashed Saucers: Evidence in Search of Proof" by which time the count was up to 92. Now the total number of people contacted connected in some way with the event is well over 130, some coming forward after the *Unsolved Mysteries* TV program broadcast first on September 20, 1989, and again on January 24, 1990.

The find in Lincoln County, New Mexico, was crashed saucer wreckage—not a Fugo or other balloon. The publicity was the result of an official press release issued from the Roswell Army Air Force Base by Walter Haut on direct orders from base commander Col. William Blanchard, head of the first atomic bombing group in the world, the 509th Composite Wing. The wreckage was brought to the base by Maj. Jesse Marcel, base intelligence officer—who was very familiar with all kinds of military and weather balloons—and by a base Counter Intelligence Corps officer as well. The cover-up was instigated shortly thereafter at both the base and at the HQ of the 8th Air Force in Fort Worth, Texas, by 8th Air Force Commander Gen. Roger Ramey on direct orders from Gen. Clements McMullen as SAC HQ in Washington, D.C. More than six firsthand witnesses described the peculiar characteristics of the wreckage. Others have described the alien bodies.

If Keel had been ethical, he would have given Major Marcel's background and conclusions instead of taking one paragraph out of context from [Whitley] Strieber's book *Majestic*.

The notion that [Frank] Scully's book *Behind the Flying Saucers* has become a part of the Roswell Incident is frankly absurd as Keel would have known if he had read Moore's 1985 paper—which thoroughly debunks Scully's book—which dealt with a supposed crash in Aztec hundreds of miles from Roswell. It may well be that the true story of what happened on the Foster ranch in Lincoln County northwest of Roswell helped shape the stories used by Scully's informants to con him. They are two separate and distinct events—one true and the other not.

Keel might even have checked the July 8, 1947, FBI memo which decries the balloon explanation. Why not talk to Walter Haut and others with firsthand involvement such as Major Marcel's son, Jesse Marcel, M.D., pilot, flight surgeon, and a member of a number of military aircraft accident investigative teams who himself held pieces of the wreckage [and believes it to be] unlike any materials he has ever handled, including during accident investigations?

Jesse Marcel, Jr., only 11 at the time of the Roswell crash, handled some of the debris his father brought home.

I surely would also like to know any basis for the statement that the mylar-like material was "indestructible" and that the plastic material "wouldn't melt." Just what did it do when exposed to heat? Major Marcel did try to burn the strange I-beams.

It seems to me that columnists should be held as accountable for their charges as authors are. Keel, unfortunately, has not been accurate in several of his pieces.—*Stanton Friedman, Fredericton, New Brunswick, Canada*

Reply to Stanton Friedman
John A. Keel

I have the uncomfortable feeling that Mr. Friedman did not read my Fugo balloon article at all. Instead, he has reacted emotionally and showered us with irrelevancies that have nothing to do with the basic facts.

Mr. Friedman has earned his living for over two decades by lecturing about the ETH and UFOs. Because of his obviously very biased interest he cannot be accused of being objective.

As a highly trained, highly experienced author and journalist with valid professional credentials spanning more than 40 years, I try to be objective. I have no "anti-ETH bias."

The governments of the world have spent billions of dollars in the past 30 years in a futile search for the existence of extraterrestrial life. Thousands of our leading scientists, radio astronomers, etc., have been involved. The results of their efforts have been widely published in every language. National magazines and major newspapers throughout the world have carried continuous articles on the search and the negative results. When some real, pro-ETH evidence appears—if it ever does—you can be sure I will be one of the first to write about it.

There is no argument that New Mexico has always been a busy area for UFO sightings, dating all the way back to the 1800s. There are thousands of UFO witnesses in that state. That's why the late Frank Scully zeroed in on it back in the late 1940s. Unfortunately, the 1980 book mentioned by Mr. Friedman was a laughable effort (and this is the opinion of many who read it) to create a sow's ear out of a silk purse. It is not uncommon for people trying to confirm a particular fantasy they are promoting by juggling and manipulating witness testimony. In this case, the debris cannot in any way be proven to be that of a flying saucer. In all these years there has never been a verifiable saucer crash, so no one can profess to be an expert on saucer composition.

It is noteworthy that when *Unsolved Mysteries* attempted to reproduce the appearance of the debris found at Roswell, as Mr. Friedman mentioned, the result was identical to the Fugo debris, which had been photographed *in situ* in many, many places in the United States. In fact, if you compare a photo of the *Unsolved Mysteries* version with any of the Fugo debris photos that are available you will find it is hard to distinguish between the two.

We must ask what qualifies Mr. Friedman to make such a grandiose statement as, "The find in Lincoln County, New Mexico, was crashed saucer wreckage..."? How many crashed saucers has Mr. Friedman personally examined? Was he there in 1947 to see this wreckage with his own eyes? What is his evidence for such a statement? For that matter, how many Fugo balloons has he seen? For many years, the aviation section of the Smithsonian Institution had a fully rigged Fugo balloon on public display. Perhaps it is still there. If so, I suggest Mr. Friedman might go and take a look at it.

Unfortunately, Mr. Friedman and his associates have had no military experience and have never worked inside the federal government. They are not even remotely qualified to comment on the workings of those bewildering organizations. They can't even speculate. They can only guess. Nor are they qualified to judge the merits of the testimony of people in the military or government. In fact, Mr. Moore has publicly confessed to the fact that he was duped, lied to, and exploited by members of the military and that he even willingly assisted them in duping other UFO investigators. Hardly a strong recommendation for his self-published "papers."

In the mid-1960s I spoke to a number of people in Roswell and New Mexico. A local historian there—I can no longer recall his name—even mentioned the Fugos and said it was the generally accepted explanation at that time. Some of the other people were obviously victims of a rather common problem—they had been "contaminated" by all the subsequent UFO books and the endless stream of UFO advocates who had visited the area since 1947. Frank Scully's book, in particular, had a very strong influence on them. It had sold in very large numbers because it was the first professionally-written book on the subject and even today it is easily available in second-hand bookstores. As I pointed out in my article, Scully's key witnesses had been vaguely discredited by an article in a men's magazine in 1952. Actually, Scully only devoted a couple of chapters to the crashed saucer stories of the 1940s and he presented them as well as he could, carefully and effectively using the same kind of material that was so clumsily used over 40 years later in the Roswell book(s).

If Mr. Friedman would bother to check the novel *Majestic*, he would find that I did not quote anything out of context. To the contrary, I quoted it exactly and at length.

He also mentions an FBI memo which was based on hearsay and was clearly intended to appeal to J. Edgar Hoover's well-known eccentricities.

Anyone who bothers to visit a good public library, or, if they live in a western state, a newspaper office, can easily verify everything that was in my short article.

As the mail response to my column has also demonstrated, there are many Fugo balloon witnesses who are still alive.

It doesn't give me much comfort to know that a nuclear physicist of Mr. Friedman's stature seriously believes in spaceships made out of rice paper, plastic, radar "chaff" and rubber cement.—*John A. Keel, New York, NY*

Roswell Revisited
Don Schmitt and Capt. Kevin D. Randle

In most of the classic cases in ufology, there are multiple answers. Occam's razor suggests that the simplest solution is probably the correct one and any answer that involves interstellar travel is probably not correct-unless it is the only one that covers all the facts.

Such is the case of the Roswell affair. There have been a number of theories about what was found by Mac Brazel in July 1947, but there is only one that seems to deal with all the facts from all the witnesses. We believe that the Fugo balloon theory, as described by John Keel, does not answer all of the questions. In his attempt to explain Roswell he didn't review the current state of the investigation.

Keel's theory is that Mac Brazel came across a rice paper Fugo some two years after the war had ended, concluding that the balloon was kept aloft by freakish winds. He says that government embarrassment about the Japanese project kept the officers of the 509th Bomb Group from revealing the real nature of Brazel's find and that Army Air Force officers at Eighth Air Force headquarters in Fort Worth substituted a weather balloon for the balloon bomb to keep the myth of American invulnerability alive.

Keel believes that the U.S. kept the Fugo balloons a secret after the war. He quotes an article published by the Smithsonian Institution in 1973 saying this was done to prevent the Japanese from knowing that their balloons were successful and then using the balloons for biological warfare. The quote was dated January 4, 1945. The Japanese abandoned the plan when they could not confirm that any of their balloons reached the North American continent.

The censorship requested of the media was abandoned after the summer of 1945 when some picnickers in Oregon (not campers in Montana as Keel wrote) examined one of the balloons and it exploded, killing six (not four as Keel wrote) of them. As a result, the war department began a "whispering campaign" to alert the public about the dangers from the balloon bombs. Programs were presented in schools, public halls, and through various civilian agencies to explain the danger of the balloons. The war department felt that such a low-key program could inform the public without letting the Japanese know the balloons were reaching the U.S.

The six deaths were the only casualties recorded in the continental United States resulting from enemy action during World War II. In 1949 a Senate committee approved a House bill to pay $20,000 to the families of those killed.

When the war ended, the secrecy was lifted. *The Washington Post* ran an article on January 16, 1946, that read, "Nine Thousand Balloon Bombs were used against the United States," and *The New York Times* of February 9, 1946, reported "Raids by Japanese Balloons."

These, plus other stories carried in local newspapers told the public about the balloon bombs. The secrecy imposed was only for the time of war and did not extend beyond the Japanese surrender in 1945. After the war there was no reason for secrecy and no evidence that the topic was still classified.

Aztec vs. Roswell

In his column, Keel points out, correctly, that the alleged Aztec, New Mexico, saucer crash has been thoroughly discredited. But the differences between Aztec and Roswell, other than their both being in New Mexico, are quite clear (see chart below).

AZTEC	ROSWELL
WITNESSES	
• No sources have been identified who witnesses any type of UFO crash near Aztec or who were involved in a recovery.	• Over 100 people were involved in some fashion near Roswell.
DOCUMENTATION	
• No documentation for this crash exists.	• The *Roswell Daily Record* of July 8, 1947, announced that the Army Air Force had captured a flying saucer. Dozens of other articles appeared in papers around the world including the *London Times*.
INFORMANT RELIABILITY	
• The informants in this case were veteran con artists who were later tried in a Colorado court for fraud in an unrelated case.	• Numerous informants corroborate each other's testimony. Informants are highly regarded and above reproach.

Other Evidence

Keel claimed that Mac Brazel found a pile of rice papers in his field which was in keeping with his Fugo theory, but never gives descriptions of the crash site. He dismisses the testimony of more than a half dozen witnesses who said the debris was scattered over a wide area—too much debris for a Fugo which was about 30 feet in diameter. In the Smithsonian Institute article that Keel quoted from there is a photo of a Fugo being examined by military and government officials. It did not come apart nor scatter debris over a large area. It is easily identifiable as a balloon.

Maj. Jesse A. Marcel, an Air Force intelligence officer who viewed the site, said that investigators had tried to burn some of the debris but could not. Rice paper would have burned easily. They tried to dent some of the larger pieces with a 16-pound sledge hammer and could not. Rice paper would have torn and some of the rubberized stuff used on a few of the balloons would have shown the effects of the hammer. Marcel had no idea what the material was.

Bill Brazel, son of the man who discovered the site, found some debris that had not been carted off to the Roswell military base. One item was described as a slender strand like a monofilament fishing line. To us it sounds like fiber optics. He found another piece of material that he could not cut with his Buck Knife, although he had used his knife in the past to cut barbed wire. He also described lead foil-like material that when wadded into a ball would unfold itself with no sign of a crease.

Bill Brazel also told us that the field where the thing crashed had been grooved. There was a shallow trench about 500 feet long but no more than 10 feet at its widest. It seemed to be a straight trench that looked as if something had hit at a low angle, bounced, and struck again. The pasture is not soft earth of the kind one would find on a farm, but solid with little top soil and a rocky substrata. Whatever hit had been traveling fast and at a low trajectory.

Capt. O. W. Henderson said that he flew some of the wreckage from

Roswell to Wright Field. He described it as something he had never seen before: dull-colored metal which was very thin and very light in weight. To us this does not sound like the remains of a paper and rubber balloon.

The day after the *Roswell Daily Record* reported that the army had a flying saucer, it carried an interview with Mac Brazel. That article stated that Mac Brazel found a weather balloon. It mentions, erroneously (according to our informants), that Brazel and Marcel took it back to the ranch house and tried to reassemble it. The article refers to balsa wood strips and aluminum foil, but there is no mention of rice paper or Japanese pictographs.

From the interviews that we have conducted over the last year we know that something unusual came down on that ranch outside Roswell. We know that it was something large enough to spread debris over a huge area. We also know that it was made of very tough material including metals, possibly fiber optics, parchment, and I-beam structures with symbols on them. Our research leads us to believe that what Mac Brazel found in the summer of 1947 was not a Japanese balloon. What it is remains a secret to this day.— *Don Schmitt and Kevin Randle*

Reply to Don Schmitt and Captain Kevin D. Randle

There are two absolutely unassailable, incontrovertible facts—not theories but solid, thoroughly substantiated, inflexible facts—about the debris found at Roswell, New Mexico, in 1947.

1) The newspapers of the day, and the testimony of the witnesses (repeated over and over again for decades after and quoted in many articles, books, radio and TV interviews) clearly described the debris as consisting of a large quantity of brown paper. Some accounts referred to it as "a truckload of paper." Some witnesses changed this to "parchment," perhaps because "parchment" sounded better…and less ordinary. The secondary material found was flexible sticks or bars of a plastic-like substance. These bars were covered with writing which, to the untrained eye, seemed like "hieroglyphics" or pictographic symbols. Samples sent to me in the 1960s were found

to contain clearly defined, unmistakable Japanese characters which translated into simple instructions such as "insert in slot B." I included some of these symbols in a paper I wrote during that period about writings often associated with UFOs. A segment of that material was published in *Operation Trojan Horse* (1970). The third and least quantitative substance found consisted of pieces of nondescript metal of various sizes, some of which appeared to be "shavings," also easily identifiable as radar "chaff" which was widely used during WW II. I wrote several articles on "chaff" during the 1960s. Others were larger pieces of very thin, very lightweight fragments with no discernible form, possibly particles of magnesium bombs which failed to explode. No machinery, instruments, or technological devices of any kind were in the Roswell debris.

This debris was not at all unique. Identical debris, with only minor variations, had been found throughout the western states from 1945 onwards at over 300 sites. It continued to appear in very isolated areas, such as forests and mountains, for the next 20 years. Its origin was known. During the last year of World War II, Japan had launched 9,000 Fugo balloons against the United States These balloons were quite large, some 33 feet in diameter, and made of rice paper—a substance so durable that traditional Japanese houses were made of it for many generations. The plastic and metal parts formed very lightweight gondolas which carried bombs—usually incendiary bombs made from magnesium, a very thin, very light metal. The balloons crossed the Pacific on the jet stream—a trip that took about three days—and eventually released their bombs at random over the United States. Some stayed aloft for very long periods after dropping their bombs and before finally crashing to the ground. In most cases, the people who found the debris knew what it was and in many instances the Army retrieved it.

There was *never* any mystery about the exact nature of the debris found at Roswell. The mystery was created by UFO advocates in the area and ill-informed local military officers who made rash public statements at the peak of the 1947 "flying saucer" wave.

Obviously, the flying saucers described by many witnesses around the world are not made of brown rice paper, aluminum, and magnesium. If the Roswell debris was from a flying saucer, it was a very strange saucer, indeed. One witness even said that there were flowers pressed into the paper. (The paper balloons were constructed by Japanese schoolchildren as a national project. The gondolas and bomb assemblies were, of course, added by adults.)

If the Roswell debris had been from a real flying saucer, its discovery would have been of major importance. Since the U.S. government had no firmly defined policy about UFOs in July 1947, the discovery would have surely been made public. The man who would have made that decision would have undoubtedly been the Army Chief of Staff. In 1947, he was five-star Gen. Dwight Eisenhower. But Ike remained silent. Years later, researchers visiting his library at Gettysburg, Pennsylvania, failed to find any documents indicating that he was even interested in the subject of UFOs. Aside from his famous anti-UFO press conference in the 1950s (he said they were "illusions, hallucinations, mistakes, and hoaxes"), he appeared apathetic. It is certain, of course, that as Chief of Staff in 1947, he was fully informed of the Kenneth Arnold sighting and other events of that year. (The U.S. Air Force was not yet a fully separate entity but was part of the U.S. Army, although plans were underway to give it an identity of its own.) We know from Ruppelt and the many documents released years afterwards that only two flying officers were assigned to investigate UFOs in June-July, 1947. They were killed in a plane crash that July.

Following the war, military budgets were slashed, personnel were cut back, and bases were closed down. The Army Air Force, as it was then called, desperately needed a new cause—an excuse to command bigger budgets. If any real evidence for the existence of flying saucers had materialized during that period you can be sure the generals would have exploited it to the hilt. They would not have concealed a crashed saucer. They would have displayed it publicly on the Capitol steps and howled: "See? This is why we need more planes, more weapons, more money!"

The Fugo balloons had been an embarrassment because our forces had not been able to stop them. Some aviation historians [check with the American Aviation Historical Society] even suspect that some of the later balloons were larger and had been manned by volunteer suicide-mission soldiers who could pick out likely targets of importance such as factories, railheads, etc. This might explain some of the persistent rumors of the discovery of bodies of small Orientals in flying suits that circulated in the Southwest after the war. Such bodies would also pose some interesting problems, including proper diplomatic/military procedures for returning them to Japan.

In 1965-66, the Pentagon refused to declassify part of the Fugo balloon files when I asked to see all the files. In 1989, author Kevin Randle asked the military to declassify the Roswell file and was bluntly told that it was none of his business. So, for whatever reason, part of the Fugo files remain a military secret 45 years after the war!

The Fugo balloon campaign is a part of the history of World War II. There have been many articles and newspaper features published on the subject, along with at least two books. Any reader who has access to a public library can easily locate some of this material. Captain Randle and his colleagues did run a library search and turned up a list of Fugo articles in a variety of national publications such as *Readers Digest, The New York Times,* etc. Actually there were hundreds of articles published between 1946–1970, particularly in regional journals and local newspapers (I wrote several of them myself). Taking photos of the debris *in situ* was routine, and a number of the pieces were illustrated with pictures of mounds of heavy paper and bits of twisted metal. The military files that I viewed in the 1960s contained several such photos. The TV show *Unexplained Mysteries* recreated the general tenure of such photos.

2) The second irrefutable fact is that nothing has happened in the

past 43 years to confirm in any fashion the notion that the Roswell debris was from a true flying saucer. If UFOs are indeed manufactured from paper, plastic, and paper-thin sheets of metal, there has not been a single incident in the hundreds of thousands of recorded UFO reports to confirm it. The most common substance found at UFO sites around the world is a purplish liquid which looks something like motor oil and dries to a cellophane-like substance. It has been repeatedly analyzed and found to be common silicon. None of this was found at Roswell—so far as we know.

Frank Scully's chief informant was a prominent oil man who carried small pieces of metal in his pocket, claiming that they were pieces of a crashed saucer. An unemployed newspaperman stole one of the pieces and had it analyzed. It proved to be nothing but ordinary aluminum. The denunciations of Scully's book are largely based upon this single fact.

The Japanese islands lacked natural resources, and the Japanese were expert at creating substitutes. They developed various plastics (early plastics were made from things like soy beans, rice, etc., while modern plastics are usually made of inflammable petroleum byproducts) and pseudo-metals for their war effort, just as the Germans, who also suffered shortages of everything, ran some of their cars and planes on hydrogen peroxide, etc.

It is highly unlikely that any of the people in New Mexico in 1947, including the military officers, were conversant with the kind of materials found at Roswell. Even today, very few people could accurately identify the heavy rice paper used in the balloon construction.

Randle also makes mention of a "monofilament fishing line." I had many samples of this in my files over the years. Ivan Sanderson used to call it "kite string." It has been analyzed and is a simple plastic. It is almost always found in great lengths—hundreds of yards—in odd places. One quantity of it turned up on a fire escape in Brooklyn. In Caldwell, New Jersey, so much of it appeared on a lawn that it had to be carted away in a truck. The late Otto Binder wrote about it in one his famous comic book stories based

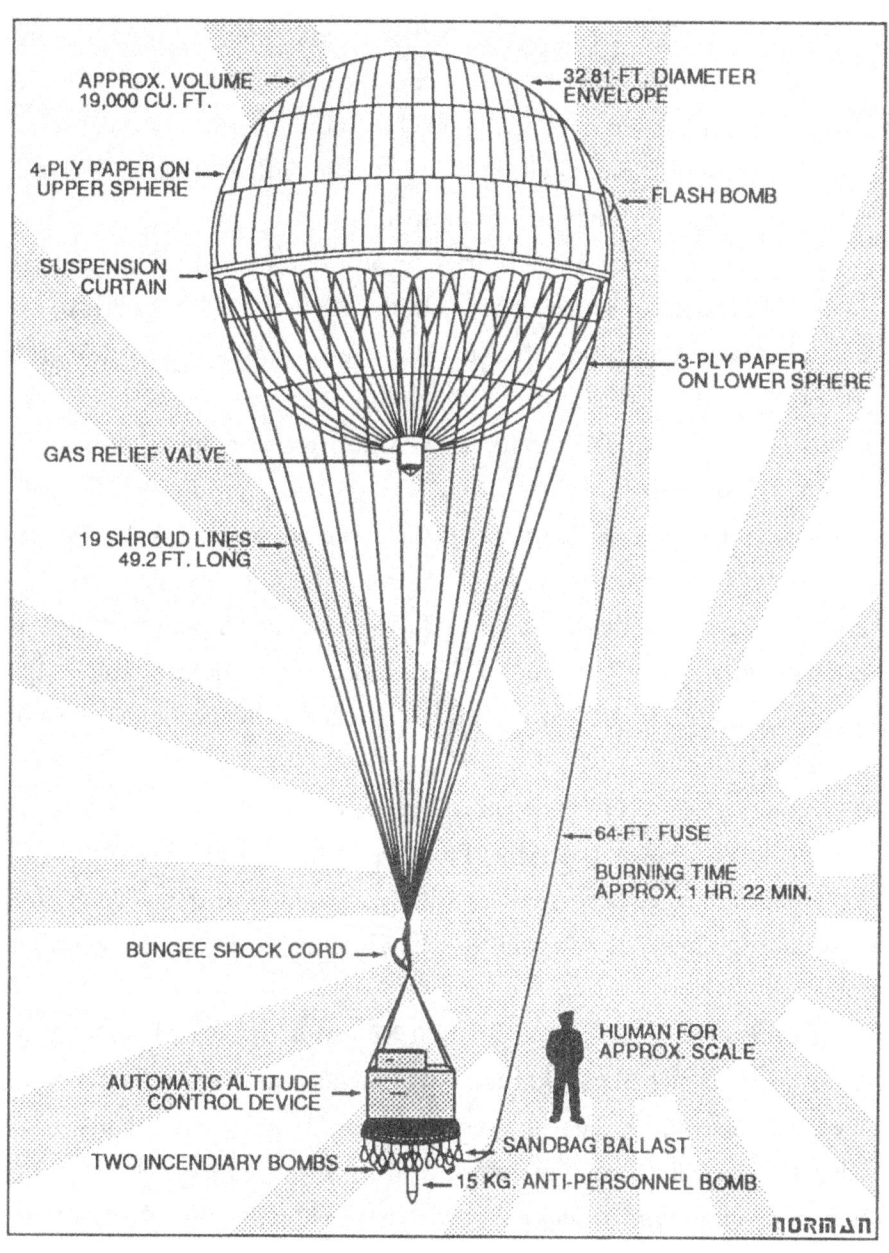

Artist's drawing of a Fugo balloon.

on this "kite string" in the early 1940s. While samples abound, no one has ever figured out what its real purpose is or where it comes from. Its appearances never seem related to UFO activity in any way. I don't recall ever seeing it mentioned before in connection with Roswell. It is rather stiff—too stiff for fishing line or kite string.

Finally, we have the very important problem of witness contamination. I wrote a number of articles on this in the 1960s and discussed it in my books. I found that it was often useless to try to investigate a case after the case had received extensive publicity or after the witnesses had been approached by local UFO buffs, many of whom are compulsive talkers who quickly try to sell the ETH and the UFO mythos. I am not surprised to hear that Captain Randle has turned up 170 alleged witnesses to a 43-year-old non-event. If he comes to New York City I can point him to another 170 Roswell witnesses in this area alone. It has been a joke for years that the legendary autopsy of a "little man" of New Mexico was attended by at least 150 people. It must have been the most crowded room in the history of autopsies.

It takes an expert interviewer to determine the extent of witness contamination in these cases. Most have told and retold their story for so long that they believe it themselves. But when you pin them down you find it is based on hearsay, on things they read long ago, or even movies they once saw.

It is true, as I have said above, that New Mexico has had many thousands of UFO sightings and incidents (such as injuries to people) over the years and some of the witnesses interviewed by Friedman, Randle, et al. have undoubtedly blurred memories which simply lump unrelated events together. In my own writings I always used the old radio formula after I discovered the limitations of the UFO audience. That formula is: Tell them what you are going to say, say it, then tell them what you said. Even so, it is very hard to get through to them. They are quite willing to accept the testimony of a solitary witness who was a small boy 43 years ago rather than deal with the hard facts. Their arguments are based on semantics.

Schmidt and Randle are engaged in the silly and hopeless tactic of trying to surmise what I "believe" on the basis of a short magazine column. If they would read my writing more carefully they would see that the column was not based on the Smithsonian booklet which came out many years after I had looked into the Fugo affair. That booklet was written by a military officer and adhered to official policy. There were many, many stories of fires started by the balloons and of personal injuries. The one that remains in my memory is the story of a group of people riding in an open car in Montana or Colorado when a Fugo bomb landed directly on them. It was clear that the bombs were more effective than the military wanted to admit. The incident at Hanford was not revealed until many years later.

I became interested in UFOs in 1944, and collected clippings and reports from New Mexico when they first occurred in the late 1940s. I have watched with amusement as the Roswell thing has been revived every few years. The story does get better as the years pass and the witnesses multiply. I suppose by 1999 there will be thousands of Roswell witnesses from that long-gone era. Here in a few pages of FATE we have seen them go from Friedman's 92 to Randle's 170.

Re: Aztec. In the 1920s and 1930s, Dr. Robert Goddard spent some of his summers near Aztec, New Mexico, then a thinly populated, very remote area. (Today it is the Aztec National Park.) There he built and tested his early rockets, financed by Sol Guggenheim, Charles Lindbergh, etc. The local ranchers were nonplussed when his strange-looking machines dropped out of the sky and then equally strange-looking people came by with old trucks to pick up the debris. As the years passed, a kind of folklore grew around Dr. Goddard's activities.

When the flying saucer phenomenon struck in the late 1940s, it was absorbed into the Goddard folklore (or vice versa) and wild tales filtered down to columnist Frank Scully about crashed saucers, the bodies of little men, etc. He relied on two key informants—a prominent oil man and an alleged scientist—far better witnesses than any Captain Randle has been able to locate 43 years later. Yet both men proved ultimately to be unreliable. The people of New Mexico love their folklore. Stories are passed from one generation to the next. Scully's accounts were scrambled in with Goddard's exploits, and it is not surprising that the Fugo balloons became a part of all this, too. In the mid-1960s, I proposed a semi-humorous article to *Playboy* centered around the Aztec/Scully legends and the episodes at nearby Farmington, New Mexico (the latter were probably the most important UFO events of the 1940s). To that end, I made many phone calls to newspapermen and witnesses in the New Mexico area, including calls to people in Roswell. If Mr. Randle would check with his 170 witnesses, he might find some who remember talking with a New York writer in the 1960s. Unfortunately for me, the great flap of March 1966 broke soon afterwards and *Playboy* asked me to write a larger article on the overall UFO scene. That's when I began more extensive investigations into the subject.

Since the early 1947 accounts of the Roswell "crash" became a part of the UFO mythology, hordes of UFO advocates passed through New Mexico, most of them stopping in Roswell to blunder into the newspaper office and molest the local people for confirmation. This still goes on. Many people have carried out religious-style pilgrimages to that barren spot, including Kevin Randle. It is akin to visiting the Grassy Knoll in Dallas and looking for spent cartridges 27 years after Kennedy's assassination.

Most objective UFO students recognized years ago that eyewitness accounts in these matters were inadequate. In the 1960s a group of witnesses in New Jersey had a remarkable sighting which I investigated most carefully. Today, nearly 25 years later, one of the principal witnesses is still writing to UFO magazines and I notice that his account has changed appreciably with age. This is because he has been endlessly interviewed by eager UFO buffs and he has also had extensive exposure to the literature. The process is insidious and sometimes imperceptible while it is happening. In the New Jersey case, his current testimony is simply invalid because it eliminates all of the really important details of the original incident.

We can assume that virtually all of the details of the discovery of the debris at Roswell are now lost, distorted by witness contamination and local legend. The brown rice paper has become "parchment" (just as the "angel hair" that rained on the people at Fatima was eventually turned into "rose petals" in the religious literature). We are expected to believe that a rational person—be he a rancher or a military officer—would willfully try to set fire to, or hammer upon, a sample that he thought was unique, one of a kind, and terribly important! Since all the key witnesses are dead—and there were only a few—there is no way to reopen the Roswell case without substantial new physical evidence.

Over 150 "crashed saucer" cases have been catalogued by UFO advocates like Tim Beckley. Unfortunately, many researchers have found that the majority of these originated in the pages of supermarket tabloids and their foreign equivalents. Others were based upon misinterpreted newspaper stories and outright hoaxes. After 43 years, not one single crashed saucer story has been verifiable. This is not because of the mythical government suppression (actually, some UFO buffs themselves censor and suppress more material than anyone else), but simply because of the obvious fact that UFOs are not crashable. In case after case, when witnesses reported something crashing into their backyard or a nearby lake or whatever, it took days or even weeks for the military authorities to show up and investigate—if they bothered at all. When a Soviet satellite crashed in Alaska in a well publicized incident a few years ago, civilians and journalists raced the military in the search for it. It is doubtful if a true crashed saucer story could be withheld from the public for very long…if at all.

So many hoaxes have been accepted by the UFO advocates (and many of them have been exposed as such repeatedly, but the advocates still accept them) that it is pointless to appeal to their logic. Nor do they remotely understand the nature of documentation and the rules of evidence. The basic facts of Roswell have always been the same.

1. Following a severe storm, the debris was found in a remote field, perhaps after having been blown there from an even more remote area. Only a very small group of people even saw the debris. Their descriptions have circulated ever since. Only one of the witnesses declared it to be the remains of a flying saucer even though he had nothing to base this conclusion upon.

2. Nothing has happened in the intervening 43 years to even slightly indicate that the debris was from a flying saucer. But everything does verify that this debris was from a Japanese Fugo balloon. The same kind of debris was found in many other places and was identified as Fugo debris. This is a matter of historical record.

The Roswell story is revived every few years by untrained, inexperienced amateur enthusiasts who are dedicated to trying to prove their personal beliefs in flying saucers. It cropped up frequently in the 1950s and 1960s in many forms, sometimes inspired by the tales of contactees or by witnesses who claimed a military background. Even a couple of alleged scientists soberly announced that they had examined the "parchment." Those people proved to be fraudulent and their motives unseemly.

Some UFO advocates have chosen to attack me rather than visit their public library and do some actual research into this matter. It is noteworthy that out of the over 80 letters my very short FATE article drew, only three were from the-incident-at Roswell-must-have-been-a-crashed-UFO supporters. The rest were from people who remembered the Fugo balloons and had some sort of experience with them.—*John A. Keel, New York, NY*

UFO Reporter
Jerome Clark
March 1991

Footnote to Roswell

I HAVE STAYED OUT of the debate between Friedman, Schmitt, and Randle on one side and my fellow columnist and old friend, John Keel, on the other as they have argued the merits of the Roswell evidence, though regular readers will have no trouble divining which side I'm on. Nonetheless, I must correct a misleading assertion Keel makes in *The Roswell Furor* in FATE's January issue.

Keel says that witnesses to the Roswell events—as of December 1990 nearly 300 had been located and interviewed—cannot be trusted because ever since 1947, when the crash took place, UFO buffs have been "molesting" them to turn a Japanese balloon into a downed spaceship. "The Roswell thing has been revived every few years," he says. In his view, in the more than four decades since something plummeted into the Brazel ranch in New Mexico, participants' testimony has been thoroughly contaminated.

This would be a respectable argument if it were based on fact. In reality, nothing of the sort ever took place as far as I have been able to determine from an extensive review of the UFO literature. While doing research for my book on ufology's early days, I have poured over not just the obscure UFO magazines and bulletins, but also the private correspondence of some of ufology's pioneering figures. The earliest printed reference I can find to the Roswell event in this literature is in 1966, in Frank Edwards' *Flying Saucers—Serious Business*. The only other reference appears the next year, in Ted Bloecher's *Report on the UFO Wave of 1947*, where it is dealt with in three paragraphs under the heading, "Hoaxes and Mistakes." Neither treatment (either Edward's positive one or Bloecher's negative one) had any impact; there are no further references to Roswell in the literature. I have been interested in UFOs since 1957. Until a few years ago I had scarcely heard of it, for the simple reason that it was never talked about.

It was forgotten until the late 1970s, when Friedman and Bill Moore learned from persons who had been on site at Roswell that the official explanation (that the object was a weather balloon), which till then had gone unchallenged, was false. None of the witnesses had been interviewed before, and Schmitt and Randle are still finding informants who, till now, never discussed the incident with outsiders.

In fact, references to any crashed-disc claims are rare in the early literature. The one specific case that got occasional, but very cautious, mention was an alleged crash in Spitzbergen, Norway, now believed to be a hoax. Ufologists held such claims in disdain (see, for example, *Civilian Saucer Intelligence Quarterly Bulletin,* September 1952, p. 5) because they associated them with the fraudulent crash stories recounted in Frank Scully's notorious *Behind the Flying Saucers* (1950). Scully's source was not, as Keel describes it, a "prominent oil man," but a lifelong confidence artist who even at the time of his death in the early 1970s was in serious trouble with the law, as he had been since the 1920s. Again, Keel to the contrary, Scully's sources were not "vaguely" but devastatingly discredited in J. P. Cahn's famous September 1952 *True* magazine expose. I urge John to read it.

Roswell Finale

Stanton T. Friedman and John A. Keel
September 1991

When John Keel wrote ("Beyond the Known," FATE, March 1990) that the object which crashed in Roswell, New Mexico, more than 40 years ago was probably a World War II Japanese Fugo balloon bomb, howls were heard throughout the UFO community. Specifically, some people who have written books and are lecturing on UFOs—and especially on the idea that the object which crashed at Roswell in 1947 was an alien vehicle—disagreed. We gave them a chance to give their comments in an article ("The Roswell Furor," FATE, January 1991) and let John Keel respond to those comments. Even so, the article ruffled enough feathers that there was a demand for one more—and final— article on the subject at this time. To try and be fair, both of the following writers were given the same amount of space, and their articles are virtually unedited. Neither writer had the chance to see the other's comments.

All of the columns in FATE are the opinions of the writers. The article that appeared in January 1991 was also the opinion of its writers. So, too, are the opinions given in the following article. They are not necessarily the opinions of FATE. FATE *would like to make the following corrections to opinions which previously appeared: (1) Mr. Friedman has earned only part of his living for over two decades by lecturing about the ETH and UFOs. (2) Contrary to Mr. Keel's claim, Mr. Friedman claims that he presents both the ETH and the anti-ETH in his lectures and books. However, Mr. Friedman's basic focus is pro-ETH. (3) Although Mr. Friedman has not been a member of the government or armed forces, he has worked on classified government sponsored research and development activities for 14 years at five companies, visited different research and development facilities and spent "weeks" at government archives. (4) Robert Goddard did not work in Aztec, New Mexico, as written by Mr. Keel. He did his rocket research in Roswell, New Mexico.*

The first writer is Stanton T. Friedman who is a lecturer on UFOs and "a major contributor" to the book The Roswell Incident *by Berlitz and Moore. Because we are not censoring anything he wrote, some of our readers may be a bit confused—a few of his comments refer to information and articles which appeared elsewhere. He stresses that his information comes from numerous interviews.*

The Real Roswell Story

Stanton T. Friedman

I WOULD NEVER HAVE BELIEVED that more than 15 years after my first conversation with Lydia Sleppy about a crashed saucer in New Mexico that I would still be pursuing the biggest story of the century, the recovery of at least two crashed saucers in New Mexico in July 1947. It has been a long, rewarding, and sometimes frustrating quest. Some key people have died. Others remain to be found. But there is no question that there is overwhelming evidence that at two different sites, about 160 miles apart, two different sets of wreckage were recovered by the U.S. government. Many witnesses, civilian and military, were strongly intimidated by government agents.

Despite the initial official press release about recovery of a crashed disc, the weather balloon radar reflector cover story was successful right from the beginning about the Brazel ranch site 75 miles Northwest of Roswell. It effectively threw a blanket in the morning newspapers of July 9, 1947, over the crashed disc story that made it into many evening papers on July 8. It came from Gen. Roger Ramey, Head of the 8th Air Force based in Fort Worth, Texas, of which the 509th Composite Bomb Wing stationed at Roswell was a very important part.

Naturally the noisy negativists have been attacking the story almost from the first time it surfaced in my documentary movie *UFOs Are Real* in 1979 and in the 1980 book to which I was a major contributor *The Roswell Incident* (Berlitz and Moore). Moore, whom I had brought into the picture, and I had done 95 percent of the research, but the book included a great deal of undocumented material from Berlitz and had essentially no public impact. By 1985 Moore and I had published six more papers. The number of directly involved witnesses had increased from 60 to 90 but except for a small community of UFO buffs, most people were blissfully unaware of the story.

The treatment in the tabloid TV movie *UFO Cover Up? Live!* in October of 1988 did little to help the cause even though it included brief appearances by Moore, heavily involved in its production, myself, and Jesse Marcel M.D., son of Maj. Jesse Marcel (Intelligence Officer for the 509th) who had with his father, handled pieces of the wreckage. Dr. Marcel is a pilot and has served on a number of military aircraft accident investigative teams and is well qualified indeed to evaluate the strange wreckage and the very unusual symbols, not Japanese, seen on some of the pieces of very lightweight, very strong wreckage. Probably what most recall is the Falcon and Condor nonsense about strawberry ice cream and the bits and pieces from early science fiction movies—ugh!

This sad spectacle led me to give up on letting Moore and Berlitz control the release of the story that I had worked so hard on, as the first to talk not only to Sleppy who tried to put the phoned-in story from Roswell on the newswire from radio station KOA in Albuquerque, but to Major Marcel and to Vern and Jean Maltais who told of their good friend Barney Barnett's story of being next to a crashed, essentially intact saucer with alien bodies in the Plains of San Agustine in New Mexico in the late 1940s. I pushed very hard, apparently successfully, to get the producers of *Unsolved Mysteries* to do the story and helped find some of the people they used besides being on briefly myself. The show ranked 12th on September 20, 1989, and 7th for the week on January 24, 1990, being seen by more than 30 million people. Many new witnesses came forth with bits and pieces of the story. Essentially none were aware of the book or our early papers or the movie scenes with Jesse. New flight crew members came forth as did many others.

Of special interest was Gerald Anderson of Missouri who had been at the Barnett site with his brother, uncle, father, and cousin, and touched one of the alien bodies before the archaeological group showed up just before the military came along in usual threatening fashion. He made site drawings after a hypnosis session with John Carpenter, a psychiatric social worker who was trained at the Menninger Clinic and has used hypnosis, in this case for memory enhancement, for a decade. Thanks to a sponsor, John and I and Gerald and my co-author Don Berliner, an old hand at ufology, were able to locate the actual site matching the drawing with a location in New Mexico, even to the windmill that was indeed there.

A very active and initially independent effort to evaluate the Roswell incident has also been conducted by Don Schmitt of the Center for UFO

Studies and former Air Force Capt. Kevin Randle, initially a skeptic. Don had asked me if there was more to do. I gave an enthusiastic "yes," but pointed out that I could not afford to spend the money on phone calls and travel that was required. When I was hot and heavy on Roswell in 1979, my phone bills frequently ran over $500 per month as they have most months the past two years. Don S. and Kevin R. have found many more crew members and have made many trips to New Mexico. They have a book due out this year, as do Don Berliner and I. We all cooperated on a project with the Fund for UFO Research that involved bringing witnesses to Washington, D.C., for a closed conference. I and either Kevin or Don Schmitt jointly interviewed and taped other important witnesses unable to go to D.C.

Not surprisingly the noisy negativists have had their knives out since 1980 and are still attacking. Noisy negativism has been characterized as one might expect by an almost complete lack of investigation, by ad hominem attacks, by proclamations, by false reasoning, by very selective choice of data. These tricks of the propagandists have characterized the intellectual bankruptcy of anti-ufology for decades. Book reviewers attacked *The Roswell Incident* for the garbage and conveniently ignored the good stuff. Even earlier, Ted Bloecher in his book on the 1947 UFO wave had dismissed the Roswell story though not getting it right. Frank Edwards in *Flying Saucers: Serious Business* used one paragraph, mostly factually in error, to pretty much dismiss the story. Neither of the two UFO encyclopedias published around 1980 even mentioned the story. Phil Klass [of CSICOP] naturally made more than 20 factual misstatements in a three-page treatment of Roswell in his book *UFOs: The Public Deceived*, as I have noted in my 1985 paper *Flying Saucers, Noisy Negativists and Truth*. Klass had, of course, not talked to any of the witnesses, reviewed none of the evidence, and hadn't been to Roswell or the Plains of San Agustine. Henry Gordon of Canada viciously attacked the story and me in articles in the *Toronto Star*. Naturally he had done no research.

John Keel is the latest to jump on the anti-Roswell bandwagon. As with Klass and Gordon, he has talked to none of the witnesses, not been on the scene, ignored all the published data, and made proclamations totally unverified by any documentation. The bashers have, of course, completely ignored the fact that the 509th was the only atomic bombing group in the world, that the stories taken independently have been consistent including testimony from Gen. Thomas Jefferson DuBose, General Ramey's Chief of Staff, who was told directly to cover up the story by SAC boss in D.C.

Perhaps out of a perverted sense of humor, Keel has tried to convert a load of small pieces of wreckage almost weightless but extraordinarily strong into a Japanese Fugo balloon somehow with witnesses supposedly stimulated by rockets launched by Robert Goddard in Aztec, New Mexico, which was also the site of supposed crashes described by Frank Scully in his long dismissed book, *Behind the Flying Saucers.* Keel's sole contribution seems to have been a possible phone conversation with an unnamed historian in Roswell in the 1960s. He claims the story was revived by loads of UFO buffs periodically beating the bushes in Roswell and that all accounts tell of brown paper as the main constituent. Great science fiction debunking but without a shred of supporting evidence.

Unfortunately for Keel's attempts to somehow mix in Scully, whose sources were con men Newton and Gebauer, as opposed to the myriad of legitimate military men and local witnesses involved in the event as have been found by my colleagues and myself along with loads of newspaper stories, Goddard worked in Roswell, not in Aztec, which is 300 miles way from Roswell. Not only is there newspaper coverage of the original official Army Air Force story (naturally ignored by Keel) but there is an FBI memo which Keel casually dismisses as having been done for the amusement of J. Edgar Hoover. The man who wrote the memo refused to talk to Bill Moore when visited and had been instructed not to say anything.

One way to judge the validity of the critics is to note their past accuracy. Klass, for example, claimed that the tradition at the White House in 1954 was the use of small elite type whereas a memo supposedly dealing with Operation Majestic 12 (ostensibly set up to deal with the Roswell crash) was in large pica type…and therefore presumably a fraud. He loudly offered me $100 for each genuine memo done in the same size and style pica type used in the memo but set a limit of ten. I did indeed collect $1,000 for providing many more than ten. The point is how could Klass, who had never been to the Eisenhower library, make such an outlandish claim, in view of the 250,000 pages of NSC material at the library, on the basis of nine items? There are many other "Klassical" boners easily avoidable with real research

Keel, too, has recently made many absurd claims about UFOs. He falsely claimed that the MJ-12 documents were frauds because all government documents of that vintage were done on 8" x 10" paper. I have visited a total of 14 archives and saw plenty of 8.5" x 11" paper. He claimed that many books in the '60s noted MJ-12 when in fact he was referring to the 5412 committee which only had a few members, not 12, and dealt with covert activities. No connection. He claimed that J. Edgar Hoover saw to it that no Jews received high level security clearances in the mid 1950s—another laugher since I am Jewish and received an AEC Q clearance in 1956.

He claimed I made a fool of myself by claiming that plutonium is used in atom bombs when it isn't. Funny, the first two atom bombs indeed used plutonium as the fissionable material. Our massive plutonium production facilities make it for bombs. He claimed I was spending full time lecturing about UFOs when since 1982 I have been mixing scientific work as a nuclear physicist with ufology.

This small list should give ample demonstration that Keel's undocumented proclamations, like Klass's, cannot be believed. He hasn't even been able to show that any Fugo balloons (as opposed to various weather balloons) were ever recovered in New Mexico even during the war as opposed to two years after. Considering the wind directions and the many mountain ranges, that is not surprising. He has provided not one article, no less all articles, saying the main material was brown paper and has not given the name of any witness he interviewed (we have named dozens) and no evidence of supposedly frequent reviving of the story by UFO buffs prior to my first interview with Major Marcel. I heard of Marcel through Don Allan, a TV station manager who was a ham radio buddy of Marcel. Neither was seeking attention. The evidence is overwhelming. There are indeed crashed saucers in U.S. possession.

The second writer is John Keel— author, lecturer and writer on the paranormal and Fortean phenomena. His arguments are based on interdisciplinary research into a variety of fields.

Roswell's Last Gasp

John A. Keel

THERE IS AN OLD country saying that states: "If it looks like a skunk and smells like a skunk, it is almost assuredly a skunk."

Over the years, many people have written to me about Roswell and I have always told them the same thing: i.e., first read Chapter Four of Charles Berlitz's book *The Roswell Incident* carefully. Then read any of the many books and articles available about the Japanese World War II bomb-carrying Fugo balloons, noting the details of how they were constructed and what they were made of. Then go back and read Berlitz again.

It's that simple.

The Roswell interviewees all described the debris found on the New Mexico ranch as being largely made of paper marked with Oriental symbols or writing. They even emphasized these two points! The Fugo balloons, you will find, were made of very special paper, laminated in four layers, that was almost impossible to tear and couldn't even be cut with scissors. Most of it was bluish on one side and silvery on the other (to reflect the heat of the sun).

It has always been easy to dismiss the Berlitz book because it is totally lacking in documentation and is heavily padded with many of the most notorious hoaxes in the UFO cult literature, particularly some the late Gray Barker's best hoaxes (he was an inveterate practical joker who enjoyed stirring up the UFO buffs).

A large part of the problem is that Mr. Berlitz, my old luncheon companion and a very busy man, innocently relied on two ardent UFO bibliophiles who totally lacked a basic background in journalism and psychology, essential subjects for this type of investigation. Interviewing people, especially people who are trying to recall events from many decades earlier, is an art that requires considerable training and experience. This duo was also plainly uninformed in such basics as aviation history, metallurgy, and fundamental field research methods.

If you own a copy of the Berlitz book, dig it out and follow along with me. First of all, the ages of the participants are completely ignored. Age is a very important piece of documentation. Look at any newspaper story and you will find the age is always given. There are good reasons for this. For example, Charles Smith, 94, tells you a lot about Mr. Smith, as does Charles Smith, 12. When you are dealing with a very old event you absolutely must give the age of each person quoted. It is a bottom rule of journalism.

In the case of Roswell, age becomes one of the most important factors. You will note that Chapter Four gives few ages, or any other journalistically necessary personal information about any of the interviewees. The interviewers cannot be accused of being overly perceptive.

Secondly, we have the problem of hearsay. For some peculiar reason, UFO buffs have a hard time understanding the nature of hearsay. Ask any lawyer friend or any professional journalist and you will find out why hearsay is totally unacceptable in any subject.

Unfortunately, the entire Roswell case is built on hearsay. That is, someone is trying to recall what someone else told them many years earlier. In some instances, they are trying to recall what someone told someone who told someone who then told them! Can you, yourself, recall in any detail a casual conversation you may have had with someone 30 years ago? Of course you can't. That's why no judge and no newspaper editor would allow your hearsay recollections to be entered into the record. As I said, it takes a very highly trained interviewer to even attempt to handle such material, and Berlitz's dynamic duo had no such qualifications.

There are so many correlations between the Fugo balloons and the Roswell debris that one could write a book about them, even using the amateurish material developed in the Berlitz tome. For example, one in every 24 balloons carried a cleverly designed tracking radio. The Japanese built three special radio stations to try to receive the signals from these radios and thus pinpoint the locations of the balloons. The radios were very, very light, for obvious reasons, and contained no tubes. Through an ingenious system of coils and condensers they sent out a brief signal once each hour. This was to conserve their very limited battery power. The radios looked like black boxes and were so finely crafted that once they were assembled they could not easily be opened again. Sort of like the famous Oriental trick boxes that we are all acquainted with.

In Frank Scully's 1950 book, *Behind the Flying Saucers*, he specifically mentions one of these radios—more than once—claiming he was shown one of them that had been found in New Mexico. Repeat: found in New Mexico. In fact, these little radios and their hourly signals are discussed in much of the early UFO literature, always with the assumption that they were otherworldly. In Berlitz's Roswell book (page 65) we learn that a man identified only as "Cavitt" found a mysterious black box in all the Oriental-inscribed paper at Roswell, couldn't figure out how to open it, and tossed it onto a truck with the rest of the debris. As shallow and incomplete as the Berlitz interviews are, there is enough material to indicate that everything found at Roswell was Fugo-related—silken shroud lines, etc. There is absolutely nothing in the descriptions to relate the debris with what we know about UFOs.

Normal investigative procedure in any event such as a plane crash, crime (particularly murder), and even archaeological digs, is to first photograph everything *in situ* before touching it. Then each piece is numbered and cataloged, noting its exact position in relation to the other pieces. Only after this has been done are the pieces carefully picked up, measured, etc., and packed away. This standard procedure was followed at many of the Fugo crash sites around the country (the balloons turned up as far east as Michigan), but it was not done at Roswell. So there was absolutely no documentation of the actual debris site. Repeat: there was absolutely no documentation of the debris site. The clearly disinterested Air Force officers just scooped the stuff into trucks and carried it off. As soon as it was picked up it became instant junk. The only surviving documentation on Roswell consists of two yellowing newspaper clippings and some photos taken by a newspaperman. The photos show officers fondling some sheets of pliable silver material which resembles exactly the paper used in the Fugo balloons. The photographer is said to have remembered that it smelled "like burning rubber" which, not surprisingly, is what the Fugos smelled like. They were heavily treated with a special chemical derived from a Japanese plant, an adhesive similar to rubber cement.

Author Charles Berlitz paid the two interviewers hard cash for their tapes, etc. They have since extracted more money from novelist Whitley Strieber, the Fund for UFO Research, and others for this poorly compiled, very questionable, and completely undocumented material. Roswell has proven to be a very profitable enterprise. In recent months, the various participants have been feuding with each other, threatening lawsuits and claiming ownership of the story. (Since Roswell was a news event, no one owns it. The various interviewees own their remembrances, not the interviewers.)

Berlitz has washed his hands of the whole affair and ended his relationships with the two interviewers years ago, citing "character differences." After writing a flop novel, *Majestic,* based on the Roswell myth, Mr. Strieber has abandoned the UFO field in dismay, disgusted with the antics of the malicious ufologists whom he has defined in a public letter as "the cruelest, nastiest, and craziest people I have ever encountered."

A novelist named Kevin Randle has re-interviewed those who allegedly knew the Roswell rancher and viewed the debris and has published a book, *UFO Crash at Roswell,* which attempts to link the Roswell debris with the legendary bodies of little men described by Scully and immortalized in Gray Barker's Hanger 18 hoax and other cultist material.

So the story goes on. Interestingly, very few UFO buffs bothered to visit their libraries and read about the Japanese Fugo project after I brought it up. Instead, they have filled their little newsletters with childish personal attacks against me and amazing dissections of my prose. Although I was careful to repeat the main points over and over in my rather brief FATE response to their earlier emotional tirades, they ignored the key points and tried to debate the meaning of words. Perhaps if they had a Ph.D. in English literature such a debate would be meaningful, but none of them are qualified to engage in a discussion of semantics. One cult magazine published on the West Coast went so far as to rewrite my FATE article about the Fugos and then put my name on it, apparently assuming (wrongly) this was the way to get around FATE's copyright. Then, incredibly, the Roswell advocates wasted their time and paper "analyzing" the bogus article and attacking me for what it did or did not contain!

I did not even know about the article until many weeks after it was published. Others have assaulted the typographical errors, which I have absolutely no control over. To save them further effort, let me state my conclusions as succinctly as possible: The Roswell affair is an easily provable misinterpretation with no link whatsoever with flying saucers. The people who perpetrated this on Mr. Berlitz, Mr. Strieber, and others in my opinion were either motivated by greed or by sheer stupidity. Or maybe by both. Considering all that has happened in the last few years, the circulation of falsified documents, etc., "misinterpretation" is no longer an appropriate word. It has become a major hoax—and a criminal hoax. Since a great deal of money has changed hands because of it, it can now be classified legally as grand larceny and there are severe penalties for that. The deliberate faking of government documents can result in a 20-year jail term.

Many aviation historians (they have a large national organization) devoted years of their lives to documenting and studying the Japanese Fugo project, preparing detailed catalogs of where the balloons came down, etc. The Smithsonian Institution had a Fugo on display for years and in 1990 published a new edition of their little souvenir booklet about the balloons. You can obtain it from the Government Printing Office or the Smithsonian. There are other editions available from aviation book clubs and bookstores. Chances are there is even an active aviation historian in your area who will be glad to read chapter four of your copy of the Berlitz book and give you his independent opinion of it.

This is simply a case of something that looked like a Fugo, and smelled like a Fugo and was turned into a UFO by a couple of over-eager saucer enthusiasts. It was accepted blindly, without question by that small but hardy band who live by what writers call "suspension of disbelief" and it has now acquired religious-like significance. Contrary to the assertions of the amateurs, there were no witnesses in 1947—that is, no one actually saw the debris come down. The man who found the debris on his ranch after a storm died in 1963 and was never properly interviewed by anyone before his death. But this is no longer a case for amateur ufologists. It is a case for the proper legal authorities and the courts.

Is this truly a "Roswell Finale"? For FATE *it is, at least for now. The main problem with this affair is that it happened over four decades ago, and as our poll reported in our July issue (in "I See By the Papers"), relatively few people were interested enough to write in and comment about what our writers had said. Some who wrote in gave their own pre-established opinions rather than commenting on the January article.*

We at FATE *believe the subject has been covered. We will not be printing more on it until some tangible evidence becomes available.*

FATE *is taking no position on what crashed at Roswell. We can say that we are sure that something crashed there. Unfortunately, reviewing books and newspapers or listening to the memories that people have of 44 years ago will not resolve the problem. Writing to* FATE *or strictly UFO-oriented magazines will not help, either. What will help is massive letter writing to your Federal representatives in Congress to reveal all of the information—including any remaining physical evidence—they have on the object that crashed at Roswell. Until they reveal this information, anything further on the subject is moot.*

UFO Reporter
Jerome Clark
November 1992

A Tale of Two Crashes

ON FEBRUARY 20, 1978, Stanton T. Friedman was in Baton Rouge, where he was to deliver a UFO lecture at Louisiana State University. While promoting the talk at a local television station, he was told he should look up Jesse Marcel. "He handled pieces of one of those things," the station's director remarked in a disconcertingly matter-of-fact tone of voice.

As every UFO buff knows by now, Marcel, now deceased but then living in a small town in Louisiana, was a retired Army officer who in 1947 served as the head of base security at Roswell Army Air Field. It was he who first recovered the debris left by the crash of an extraordinary flying object which came down on a ranch near Corona in remote Lincoln County, New Mexico.

The unraveling of the Roswell cover-up begins with Friedman's first interview with Marcel. It would not be, by a long shot, his last interview with someone connected with the story. It would be the beginning of an investigation which continues to this day. The early results were reported in *The Roswell Incident* (1980), written by ufologist William L. Moore (who had joined Friedman in the investigation) and popular occult author Charles Berlitz. In 1991 Kevin D. Randle and Donald R. Schmitt's *UFO Crash at Roswell*, based on an independent inquiry by the Center for UFO Studies (CUFOS), was released. That same year saw the publication of a 146-page monograph, *The Roswell Report*, edited by George M. Eberhart and published by CUFOS.

Cosmic Collision

Friedman finally has his own book, *Crash at Corona: The U.S. Military Retrieval and Cover-up of a UFO* (Paragon House, 217 pages, $19.95). Written with aviation journalist Don Berliner, it starts out with a chronicle of by now familiar events and anecdotes, recounting them in a flowing, readable style. Here and there a heretofore-unreported item shows up just as the knowledgeable reader's attention has started to flag. To be fair, much of this material would not be familiar if Friedman hadn't uncovered it and reported it (or allowed others to report it) long before he landed a book contract. On the other hand, much of the story came to light through the mammoth labors of Randle and Schmitt, who are only stingily credited here—for reasons I shall explain in due course.

No one denies that Friedman deserves to have his name on the cover of a Roswell book, and nobody begrudges him the unavoidable treading over well-beaten paths. After all, to some considerable extent he is following his own footprints. But what has made *Crash* a deeply controversial book is what happens when, as it does eventually, it departs from the familiar trail and leads readers in a startlingly new direction. Alone among Roswell chroniclers, Friedman and Berliner maintain that a second craft crashed on the Plains of San Agustin, 150 miles to the west of Corona. This second craft, they contend, probably collided with the Corona vehicle.

Where did such a fantastic notion come from? It takes its inspiration from the claims of a Springfield, Missouri, man named Gerald Anderson, of whom not a single ufologist had heard prior to January 1990. Today, as the most famous-or notorious-UFO claimant of the moment, he is at the center of a furious debate.

Anderson surfaced after a January 1990 rerun of a Roswell segment on NBC's popular docu-drama series *Unsolved Mysteries*. The show's production company referred him to Randle, who soon spoke with him over the phone. Subsequently that phone conversation would itself become the subject of considerable discussion. In any case, by the time Randle put down the receiver, he had begun to suspect that what he had just heard was not the truth.

For his part, Friedman hastened to send Anderson a packet of material detailing what he and other researchers had learned about the Roswell event. He interviewed Anderson for the first time shortly afterwards. Not surprisingly, Friedman's critics would make much of this apparent tutoring of a witness. Even more controversially from the critics' perspective, Friedman urged Anderson to break contact with Randle and to cooperate only with him. From then on Anderson ignored Randle's letters and phone messages, and the two would have no further communication. From this unpromising start has erupted one of the most contentious, bitter, and personal conflicts to afflict UFO research in years. To understand what it is all about, it is necessary to place Anderson's claims in context.

Death on the Plains

In 1978 Friedman learned of a story told by Grady "Barney" Barnett, a U.S. Soil Conservation Service engineer, to a few trusted friends. Barnett, unfortunately, could not be interviewed directly; he had died nine years earlier. According to his friends, Barnett claimed that during the summer of 1947, while working on the Plains of San Agustin, he spotted a "large metallic object" stuck in the ground. With a group of archaeologists who had arrived a short time before, Barnett gaped in wonderment at the bodies of four humanoid beings who lay nearby. In short order a group of Army men showed up and ordered the civilians off the site, warning them never to tell anyone what they had seen.

From everything investigators have been able to determine, Barnett was an honest man. He told this story separately—and consistently—to a small number of trusted friends, all of whom say they believed him. Much later the diary of Ruth Barnett, Barney's wife (also deceased), surfaced after her niece Alice Knight found it. The diary confirms that Barnett worked on the Plains in early July 1947 but says nothing about a flying-saucer crash.

Though they could not verify Barnett's crash story, Moore and Berlitz used it in their book, as would most other subsequent writers on Roswell. It figures in their imaginative recreation of the events leading to the crash: "Somewhere north of Roswell, the saucer ran into a lightning storm... [It] made a course correction to the south-southwest, was struck by a lightning bolt, and suffered severe on-board damage. A great quantity of wreckage was blown out over the ground [to fall near Corona], but the saucer itself, although stricken, managed to remain in the air for at least long enough to get over the mountains before crashing violently to the ground in the area west of Socorro known as the Plains of San Agustin."

Living Proof

But by 1985 Moore had just about given up on the San Agustin story. His effort to find other witnesses, notably members of the alleged archaeological team, had turned into little more than an "exercise in frustration." In a paper for the MUFON 1985 UFO Symposium Proceedings, he noted the "marked lack of additional corroborating accounts... [T]he Barnett investigation seems to have reached an insurmountable impasse from which nothing in the way of new evidence seems likely to emerge in the foreseeable future."

Meanwhile, even as San Agustin witnesses remained elusive, the body of testimony from persons (including everybody from local ranchers to Air Force generals) who were directly or indirectly involved with the Corona event grew impressively. Investigators even located individuals, both military and civilian, who said they had viewed the remains of the vehicle's crew. But even they did not place these bodies on the Plains of San Agustin. Longtime residents of the Plains deny that a UFO crash took place there.

In their book, Randle and Schmitt, still unwilling to abandon the Barnett story, speculated unpersuasively that Barnett had encountered the bodies at Corona but claimed otherwise to "cover his tracks." Earlier this year, in an article in *International UFO Reporter* ("Second Thoughts on the Barney Barnett Story," May/June issue), they withdrew the suggestion. They wrote, "We can only conclude that Barnett was not on the [Mac] Brazel ranch," where the debris was found near Corona. "At the same time no good evidence supports the contention that a UFO crashed on the Plains of San Agustin."

Even so, they acknowledged, "During our investigation we found nothing to suggest that Barnett was a practical joker… Nothing in his background suggests he would have made up such a story. In fact, he told neighbor Harold Baca that he was convinced his throat cancer was the result of his having breathed irradiated air while at the crash site. Certainly this does not sound like the sort of detail a man would invent."

Nonetheless, in the absence of additional evidence, Randle and Schmitt felt they had no choice but to let the story go. An account this incredible needs more than one witness, however sincere that one witness may seem to be, if it is to be taken seriously. Actually, in this instance there was less than one witness. The long-dead Barnett's account survived only in the memories of persons to whom he had related it. No knowledgeable investigator had a chance to talk with him face to face and ask him all the questions that must be asked—questions that, sadly, may never find answers.

In short, like hundreds of other unsubstantiated crashed-saucer anecdotes, Barnett's story begins in promise and ends in ambiguity. From this point of view it turns out to be an intriguing but unverifiable anecdote ultimately of more interest to the folklorist than to the ufologist.

Or is it something more than that? It is if we credit what Gerald Anderson has to say. If Anderson is speaking truthfully, the Barnett story must be viewed in a whole new light because at long last we have a living San Agustin witness. To Friedman, Anderson's account not only backs up Barnett but establishes that two UFOs plowed into each other before descending on Corona and San Agustin in July 1947. Or is it a whole lot less than that?

Beyond the Known
John Keel
April 1993

Return of the Fu-gos

Over 200 FATE READERS have now written to me regarding the cult misrepresentation of the wartime Japanese fu-go balloons which I discussed in these pages about three years ago. Most described their personal sightings in 1945 and how military officers or FBI agents urged (ordered) them not to discuss what they had seen. Some maintained their silence for decades until they saw my brief article.

Those wartime "Men In Black" were mighty persuasive! There must be thousands of other wartime witnesses out there who do not read FATE and are still keeping their experiences to themselves.

When I submitted the piece to FATE, I included a long list of books and references which the FATE editors chose not to print. (They also shortened my original text somewhat.) I did, however, send out copies of that list to everyone who bothered to write and ask for it. Since then, there have been several new additions to the literature. Keep in mind that most of these books are somewhat technical, quite expensive, and hard to find. The best places to look for them are through the various aviation book clubs and military book stores.

For you late subscribers, here's a summary of the fu-go balloon situation: Near the end of World War II the Japanese built and launched 9,000 bomb-carrying balloons against the United States. Hundreds of them actually managed to drift across the Pacific on the Jet Stream and drop their bombs on the U.S., Canada, and Mexico, causing numerous forest fires and a few deaths and injuries.

It sounds absurd today, but each balloon was the size of a three-story house, contained about 90,000 cubic feet of hydrogen gas (the Japanese didn't have any helium), and was made of a special paper. Very lightweight metals, plastic, and wood were used in the construction of their bomb-carrying gondolas. One balloon in every 24 was equipped with a clever radio that transmitted a beep every hour so the Japanese could try to track its progress.

If you ever wander into an Oriental souvenir store you might find a package of "rice paper" (it is not made from actual rice) for sale. Then you can see just how tough some of this paper can be. It is almost impossible to tear it. Some kinds can only be cut with special instruments. The fu-go balloons were made with this very resilient, non-porous paper laminated in four layers, some of it coated with a silvery finish to reflect the heat of the sun. The balloon panels were glued with a special substance made from a Japanese plant. The paper had to be leakproof because hydrogen gas is volatile and difficult to contain. The result was huge balloons that were almost indestructible.

Screaming Monkeys

Three different, unrelated people wrote to tell me of almost identical experiences. Each saw a low-flying balloon somewhere in the U.S. in 1945 with a gondola containing a living creature. At a distance, all three thought they were seeing a "screaming monkey." When the balloon came closer, they realized it was really a very small man wearing some kind of headgear, probably radio headphones. The poor fellow was clearly agitated. Two of the letter writers noted that he had a very angry expression, even a hatefilled one. He appeared to be an Oriental.

Soon after the balloon bounced away, disappearing over a hill or the horizon, one or more Jeeps filled with soldiers suddenly roared onto the scene, apparently in hot pursuit. Two of the witnesses said they heard shots a few minutes later. All three reported that the Jeep(s) came back and a military officer stopped and warned them sternly to forget what they had just seen. "Don't even discuss this with your parents," one was told.

History tells us that the Japanese had, in fact, planned to launch manned fu-go balloons against the U.S. from submarines surfaced a few miles offshore. This would account for the three eyewitness reports. It would explain many other things, too, such as the persistent rumors in the 1940s about the bodies of small, Oriental-looking men in flight suits that were supposedly recovered in various western states.

Author Frank Scully made two trips to New Mexico in an effort to track down these rumors for his book *Behind the Flying Saucers* (1950). Hundreds of reporters and investigators followed him. They all found plenty of hearsay but no actual evidence.

Mr. Mark Gardner, an ace fortean, once interviewed some fishermen who claimed to have seen a Japanese sub sending up balloons off the coast. However, they pinpointed the date as being 1947, not 1945, making the whole incident rather unlikely.

Although most of the fu-gos self-destructed, many crashed to earth intact and were found later by mystified farmers and hikers. The most recent find was in North Dakota in 1990, 45 years after the balloons had been launched! Remains of these balloons have been found as far east as Michigan.

Top Secrets Revealed

No actual documentation remains at this late date, but it is very possible that one or more Japanese balloonists attempted the 3,000-mile flight across the Pacific to see if manned balloons were practical. If such a project was launched, they would have selected the smallest, lightest volunteers available (just as our modern astronauts are small men). It is also likely that they might have expired during the trip, frozen in the high altitudes or suffering from lack of oxygen. If their bodies ever came down anywhere their complexions would have been very odd, discolored by the cold, and so on.

If even one such volunteer balloonist attempted the trip and crashed, we would have the answer to all those rumors and legends which persist to this day.

Wartime Weirdness

In the 1930s, Dr. Robert Goddard conducted his early rocket experiments in an 18,000-acre "field" in New Mexico, backed by Sol Guggenheim, Charles Lindbergh, and others. The Nazis stole Goddard's patents and designs, incorporating them into their V-2 rocket bombs. After the war, we salvaged 100 intact V-2s and brought them to the United States—to New Mexico, naturally. There, a handful of military men and German scientists tinkered with them for several years. Small animals and monkeys were given rides in some of those rockets, adding to all the rumors and legends circulating in New Mexico. In the 1940s, it was the most sparsely populated state, with fewer than 800,000 people, largely Indians and Hispanics. Even today, over 40 years later, the state has only 1,500,000 hardy souls.

We not only developed the atomic bomb in New Mexico, we were carrying out all kinds of weird projects. The ejection pods for fighter planes were developed there. Anyone who saw one of these early pods dropping from the sky, with a human-shaped dummy aboard, had a story to tell his grandchildren years later. We were also training bats to haul incendiary bombs through the night, the idea being that they could be released over

Japan and set fire to the flimsy Japanese houses. (See *Bat Bomb: World War II's Other Secret Weapon* by Jack Couffer.)

We didn't even know about the jet stream until the fu-gos began to arrive. After the war, we hastily began a series of top secret tests near Goddard's old base in Eden Valley, New Mexico, launching "Sky Hook" balloons into the upper atmosphere. We found that the jet stream looped around the world and that balloons launched in New Mexico would end up over Russia!

In other words, we set up our own fu-go balloon program. However, our balloons were much bigger than the fu-gos and carried radios and cameras instead of bombs. They were so huge they were code-named "Moby Dick." Eventually we sent thousands of Moby Dick balloons over Russia in those pre-U2 spy plane days. (See *The Moby Dick Project* by Curtis Peebles.)

Homebuilt UFOs

Now we know that many of the UFO sightings from the late 1940s were, in fact, secret government tests of various kinds. Many of the sightings of 1945 in the Western states were undoubtedly fu-go balloons. Later sightings, particularly in Europe, were Moby Dicks.

All these silvery balloons certainly added to the confusion and the U.S. military eventually learned to take advantage of the situation and issue false UFO reports to cover up nuclear accidents (see such books as *The History of the U.S. Nuclear Arsenal* by James Norris Gibson) and other official bungling. Small wonder that the UFO scene became a chaotic mess. Adding to the mayhem, a Hungarian airliner collided with a swarm of Moby Dicks in 1955, killing all on board and creating an embarrassing international incident.

I took a special interest in the fu-gos in the 1960s, particularly after people began sending me pieces of debris which they thought were from outer space. The strange writing on this mysterious junk always proved to be

Japanese.

Oldtimers will recall that I wrote a number of articles mentioning the fu-gos, such as my piece "The Myth of UFO Censorship" which appeared in the April 1969 issue of Ray Palmer's *Flying Saucers* magazine. It began with a quote from fu-go expert Robert C. Mikesh. Mr. Mikesh was the author of the book *Japan's World War II Balloon Bomb Attacks on North America*. It is one of the few fu-go books still in print.

Mr. Mikesh retired last year as director of the aviation museum of the Smithsonian Institution. I mention this because the Smithsonian had a fully rigged fu-go balloon on public display for many years. Seven other museums, such as the one in Klamath Falls, Oregon, also have fu-go displays.

Anyone who wants to see for themselves the kinds of paper and metal used in their construction can easily track them down. Two other museums in Canada also have fu-go exhibits.

In 1990, a Japanese television network sent a camera team to the U.S. to interview surviving fu-go witnesses for a documentary that was aired in Japan on December 7, 1990. Interesting timing.

Another fu-go expert is Bert Webber of Medford, Oregon. He has made the subject a life-long pursuit and has even met and interviewed the Japanese scientists and military men who were behind the fu-go project. His book, *Silent Siege II*, is still in print and is the best available work on this whole fascinating episode. It sells for around $35.

If you were around in 1945 and lived in a Western state, you may have a fu-go story of your own. Perhaps you saw a mysterious explosion in the sky or watched a silvery balloon drift downwards. Maybe a stern military officer even ordered you to keep your mouth shut. If you had any experience(s) of this sort I would like to hear about it.

If you saw one of those "screaming monkeys" clad in a flight suit and wearing headphones, I would really appreciate all the details.

Of course, we understand that it is next to impossible to recall all the accurate details of something that happened nearly half a century ago. Don't try to fill in the gaps. Just tell us whatever you can remember. Maybe we can piece the Big Picture together from fragments of information from many people.

UFO Chronicle
J. Antonio Huneeus
June 1994

Roswell Blues (Part I)

NEW MEXICO REPRESENTATIVE Steven Schiff recently reviewed the 1947 Roswell UFO crash and was baffled by the lack of response from the Department of Defense. There can be little doubt that the story of a UFO crash at a remote ranch near Roswell, New Mexico, in early July 1947, has become an American legend. It is no longer merely one among hundreds of obscure UFO tales circulating within the ufological community.

It is a story that has slowly crept into the mass media and has even reached the halls of Congress. Four books and countless articles and TV programs have been devoted to the case—the latest one, *The Truth About the UFO Crash At Roswell* (M. Evans & Co.) by Kevin Randle and Donald Schmitt, is scheduled to appear as a *Showtime* movie later this summer. This once sleepy Southwestern town is now booming with displays of the incident, including two local UFO museums.

Last January 13th, the *Albuquerque Journal* broke the story that Representative Steven Schiff (Republican-N.M.) had requested the General Accounting Office (GAO) to look into the Roswell affair. The following day the story was confirmed in *The Washington Post*'s influential "Federal Page" under the headline of "GAO Turns to Alien Turf in New Probe," which quoted a GAO spokeswoman acknowledging that "only one investigator had been assigned" to the case.

Congressman Schiff provided further background a few weeks later during an interview with CBS radio talk show host Gil Gross. A resident of Albuquerque for 25 years, Schiff said that "I heard of the Roswell incident you described many years ago; I did not know how prominent it was to people who study these matters."

Phil Klass and others have suggested that Schiff's interest may have been sparked by his district director and former legislative director Mary Martinek, who happens to be married to Karl Pflock. Pflock is a former government official and UFO researcher who has conducted his own independent investigation of Roswell.

The story was reported in the *Albuquerque Journal* under the subtitle of "Schiff Denies Prompt From Aide's Spouse," but according to the *Journal*, "his interest was sparked by a 'flurry' of letters from constituents."

Schiff explained that it's routine for Congressmen to get letters from the public requesting assistance in obtaining information from various government agencies. "I felt that this all along was a routine matter," said Schiff to CBS radio, "but I just have to say this much, the way the Department of Defense has responded has not been routine."

We have obtained copies of the correspondence between Schiff, the DOD, and the National Archives. In a three-page letter to then Secretary of Defense Les Aspin, dated March 11, 1993, Schiff outlined the known facts.

These include the discovery of the debris field near Corona by rancher William "Mac" Brazel and the well-documented chain of events involving Chaves County Sheriff George Wilcox. Later Maj. Jesse Marcel, the intelligence officer at the Roswell Army Air Force base, and Capt. Sheridan Cavitt, a counter-intelligence officer, also got involved.

Government Accountability

Finally, the base public information officer issued a press release announcing the recovery of a flying disc, and Gen. Roger Ramey, Commander of the Eighth Air Force in Fort Worth, Texas, debunked the whole affair as the "remains of a weather balloon and its Rawin radar target."

"Similarly documented testimony given by a number of still living and seemingly credible witnesses," continued Schiff's letter, "suggests that, in addition to the cover story, Federal authorities sought to intimidate witnesses and their families into silence."

After pointing out "the inconsistency between repeated official denials and the public record and testimony of those involved," Congressman Schiff finally requested the Secretary to "promptly arrange to brief and provide me with a written report providing a current, complete, and detailed description and explanation of both the nature of what was recovered and all official actions taken on the matter."

Before you get the wrong idea of Schiff as some kind of UFO crusader, you ought to know that he characterizes his own personal opinion as coming "a little closer to the description of a skeptic rather than a believer." He said to Gil Gross that "my view is still that in fact it [Roswell] could have been a weather balloon, accompanied by a public relations fiasco both in 1947 and, if I may say, now, or some other explanation of that kind."

Nevertheless, he added that "the issue to me, however, is government accountability. I think that people who want to see government records are entitled to see government records or to get an explanation of what happened to them, regardless of the subject matter."

Schiff's request was routed to the Air Force, which directed him to the National Archives. The Director of the Archives' Textual Reference Division, Michael McReynolds, eventually told him what every Roswell researcher has known for years: that there is no "documentation relating to this event [Roswell] in Project Blue Book records" and, moreover, that they have "received numerous requests" about the matter.

Congressman Schiff now says that he's baffled by the whole runaround. He told Gil Gross: "I was not told that we have a file that's classified, I was simply referred to an agency which—now that I know the prominence of the Roswell incident—I have to believe the Department of Defense knew very well that I wasn't going to find anything in the National Archives when they sent me there twice…It's difficult for me to understand even if there was a legitimate security concern in 1947, that it would be a present security concern these many years later."

Readers shouldn't get the impression that a full-fledged government investigation of what transpired in Roswell 47 years ago is currently going on, however. A few discreet inquiries revealed that there isn't any urgent priority in the GAO probe. It still consists of only one researcher, who is looking into something like Air Force procedures in handling aircraft accidents back then.

On the other hand, if there are any official records related to Roswell, we can predict that it's only a matter of time before they are found and released. The trend these days is definitely in the direction of opening all the musty secret files from the Cold War, as recent disclosures of radiation experiments with human beings have shown.

Moreover, *The New York Times* reported on its front-page last March 18 that President Clinton had instructed the National Security Council to draft an order to change government secrecy rules from the restrictive executive order issued by President Reagan in 1981. "The order would require the automatic declassification of secret documents after 25 years," reported the *Times*. This obviously includes Roswell's time frame.

Selling Roswell

Meanwhile, selling the Roswell legend in Roswell itself continues at full speed. Just as we go to press, Kevin Randle and Don Schmitt were in town to launch their new book with a press conference at the International UFO Museum and Research Center, followed by a packed lecture in the Pearson Auditorium.

There can be little doubt that the revival of the old Corona crash—long forgotten since General Ramey's famous press conference of July 8, 1947—has become a miracle for the local economy. An official at the museum told us that they have had 23,000 visitors since their opening in April 1992, and are bracing for many more with the publicity expected from the new Roswell book and *Showtime* movie.

Not surprisingly, the museum's President, Walter Haut, and Vice-President, Glenn Dennis, played key roles in the interpretation of the original events, though neither were firsthand witnesses to the UFO debris or its alleged occupants. Haut, a friendly man whom I met and interviewed during a visit to Roswell in 1991, was the young lieutenant who issued the famous press release announcing the recovery of a flying disc.

Dennis was the mortician who was told of alien bodies at the base by a nurse who had been present during one of the examinations. Unfortunately, the nurse was transferred shortly thereafter and supposedly died later in a plane crash, so no corroboration for that particular account has been produced so far.

During the 1991 visit I also met John Price, owner of the Roswell UFO Enigma Museum, located near the entrance to the old Roswell base, and its research director Clifford Stone, a retired Army sergeant who can be best described as Roswell's resident ufologist. Price operated a small UFO exhibit attached to his "Outa Limits" video store.

He told us recently that he had just expanded the museum to 4,400 square feet to accommodate new exhibits. Needless to say, both museums sell all kinds of souvenirs such as T-shirts, mugs, and books, etc.

I have nothing against the welfare of the people of Roswell, but one can draw at least a parallel with what Nessie did for the tourist economy of Loch Ness in Scotland over the last six decades.

I could march along with the bulk of American ufology and praise the glories of the Roswell incident, but I wouldn't be doing my job as a journalist if I told you that all's well in the Roswell camp. Although I've never been one of the primary investigators, I've observed closely how several teams of ufologists have tried to document the case since the late '70s, ripping each other apart in the process.

I published a long article about Roswell in a New York newspaper back in July 1982, seven years before the CUFOS team of Randle and Schmitt even began their investigation. I've met all and interviewed most of the Roswell authors and I've interacted with the competing teams.

The story of the Roswell investigation is more byzantine than a spy plot, with researchers changing alliances, producing alleged "top secret" documents, accusing each other, and questioning aspects of their respective stories at different stages. Each successive team has carefully skirted around the contributions of the previous one, managing at times to even erase certain names or papers.

None of this is pretty, yet it has to be faced if one honestly tries to make sense about everything that has been claimed and published on Roswell. While all the books more or less agree on the sequence of events from the discovery of the debris field in Corona to General Ramey's press conference in Fort Worth, all of which are fairly well documented in the public record, the scenarios differ considerably with regards to the location, date, and details of the crash of the UFO's main section and its alleged alien crew.

For years this was believed to have occurred some 150 miles west of Roswell in the Plains of San Agustin. The problem was there were no firsthand witnesses to this location until a man by the name of Gerald Anderson appeared on the scene, offering an exciting account of being right on the spot of the crash in the Plains with his family when he was five years old.

Anderson had a compelling story to tell which many in the ufological community believed implicitly. His testimony became the subject of a heated controversy in the UFO press, but the man was finally exposed as a forger and a liar.

Don Berliner, co-author with Stanton Friedman of *UFO Crash at Corona* (1992, Paragon House), where the Anderson story was reported as factual, had this to say about the Plains scenario in a recent telephone interview: "We don't have firsthand witnesses, the case is very weak for the Plains. Anderson is a known liar and as far as I am concerned, you can't believe any word he says."

One would think that Roswell researchers would learn the lesson and be extra cautious the next time some guy comes along singing stories of having seen dead aliens. Unfortunately, that doesn't seem to be the case. Next month we'll provide a critical examination of the evidence offered by Randle and Schmitt in *The Truth About the UFO Crash at Roswell*.

Linda Update

Our predecessor in this column, Jerome Clark, wrote us to make a correction regarding a statement in the February issue of FATE that CUFOS had endorsed the Linda Cortile abduction as "the case of the century." Clark wrote that "views on the case, in fact, range from dubious to unprovable" among his CUFOS colleagues and that, "for that matter, we don't think any abduction case constitutes, or even could constitute, the case of the century—unless it occurred, of course, at high noon on the White House lawn."

I apologize for having misconstrued CUFOS' view on this matter, but disagree with Clark in his final statement. If—and it's a big if—Linda's abduction was indeed witnessed by Perez de Cuellar (Jim Schnabel in his new book *Dark White* goes even further, reporting that Budd Hopkins and Linda believe that Cuellar was also abducted), then it would qualify as "the case of the century."

As Secretary General of the United Nations, Cuellar was then the titular head of the world, so the case conjures all kinds of images of "take me to your leader." The problem, of course, is proving it.

UFO Chronicle
J. Antonio Huneeus
July 1994

Roswell Update (Part II)

B Y THE TIME YOU READ this column, two new works on the famous 1947 Roswell UFO crash mystery will be available. The first is *The Truth About the UFO Crash At Roswell*, a handsome 251-page book by Kevin D. Randle and Donald R. Schmitt published by M. Evans & Co., with photos, appendices, notes, bibliography, and index.

The second is the monograph *Roswell in Perspective*, by Karl Pflock, published by the Fund for UFO Research. Considering the prior history of the Roswell investigation, it shouldn't come as a surprise that both works are quite at odds with each other.

Pflock's monograph was not yet available as we go to press, but we were able to get a summary of his research and conclusions in a telephone interview with the author, who also provided an update on the General Accounting Office (GAO) probe requested by New Mexico Congressman Steven Schiff.

"This book is going to annoy a large number of people," wrote Randle and Schmitt (R&S) in their book's afterword, adding that, "we are taking the conventional wisdom about the Roswell UFO crash and tossing it out. We are beginning again, using the testimony and the documentation that we have been able to discover during the last four years of intensive investigation."

By "conventional wisdom" R&S implied primarily the date of the crash, which in all the previous books (including their own 1991 *UFO Crash at Roswell* paperback) was placed on the night of July 2, 1947. Now, R&S propose the night of July 4 as the UFO impact date, based on the testimony of two alleged firsthand witnesses to the crash of the main vehicle, as well as some lights in the sky seen by three independent sets of witnesses during the same night.

Other details like the number of aliens in the UFO—five instead of four; the shape of the craft—triangular instead of a saucer; and the timeline of the discovery of the debris field in Corona by rancher W. W. "Mac" Brazel, as well as aspects of the recovery operation, have also necessarily changed with the new date.

There was never much agreement among the various teams of researchers regarding the second crash site, as opposed to the by now well documented debris field at the Foster ranch near Corona. The first 1980 book by Charles Berlitz and William Moore, *The Roswell Incident*, as well as the third one by Stanton Friedman and Don Berliner, *UFO Crash at Corona*, proposed the second crash site 150 miles away in the Plains of San Agustin.

With the exception of Friedman, however, few researchers are currently defending the Plains hypothesis following the Gerald Anderson affair. R&S made the case in their first book that the second site, located quite near the first one, was only discovered on the afternoon of July 8 by a military plane surveying the area after the debris field in Corona had been secured. The information on that particular operation, however, was very sketchy.

Not so in their new book. R&S present two star witnesses, one Jim Ragsdale and a retired military officer with the pseudonym of Steve MacKenzie, who provide plenty of details about the second site. Both the civilians—Ragsdale and his female companion Trudy Truelove, as well as a group of archaeologists under Dr. W. Curry Holden from Texas Tech University—and the military were on the scene by the morning of July 5.

While the book is fairly entertaining and will probably provide a good introduction to those not familiar with the case, I found the evidence for their new scenario quite weak.

R&S seem to put enormous confidence on the testimonies of Ragsdale and MacKenzie but provide very little, if any, information and documentary evidence on their backgrounds both then and now. In other words, they don't make a good case for the reliability and trustworthiness of their witnesses, which would seem crucial considering the importance of their claims. We are supposed to believe in what these witnesses have to say simply because R&S did.

The second set of problems is what I would term the "deathbed confessions." Stanton Friedman characterized it best when he said that the Roswell investigation was "a race against the undertaker."

Serious Problems for the Investigators

Obviously this is nobody's fault although it creates serious problems for investigators. Thus, after much diligent research by Tom Carey who searched meticulously for the fabled archaeologists who had reportedly discovered the main crash site during a routine field expedition, professor Holden was located.

He was 96 years old, however, and, when interviewed in late 1992 just a few months before his death, Holden said "he could remember nothing about the event, other than that he had been there and had seen it all." R&S make much of this last assertion that he "had seen it all." But what exactly did he see? We'll never know unless some written records are found in the professor's papers.

Similarly, the provost marshall of the 509th Bomb Group stationed at the Roswell base in 1947, Maj. Edwin Easley, was initially reluctant to talk about the incident because of national security. Then shortly before he died, Easley supposedly confirmed "that the craft had been extraterrestrial in origin" and that he had seen the bodies. "He had been close enough to them to know they weren't human," wrote R&S, adding that "he called them 'creatures.'"

All this is fascinating but the authors provide very little information in their notes regarding this and other interviews with witnesses, such as whether recordings exist, duration and number of people present during the interviews, etc. The lack of testimony in quotation marks and additional references becomes particularly acute in the extremely sketchy information that R&S provide about the doctors supposedly involved in the autopsies.

I don't enjoy being critical toward this book, yet the ufological community will have to come up with an airtight case if they ever hope to prove the extraterrestrial reality of the Roswell crash. This quality is what the book is lacking.

Enter Mr. Pflock

"We are now confronted with the work of a former CIA employee who in November 1992, injected himself into the Roswell case," wrote R&S in their afterword, predicting that the coming weeks will see "politically motivated" criticism of their book. The man in question is Karl Pflock, a former CIA and DOD official who lives in Albuquerque, where his wife works for Congressman Schiff.

Those interested in his background can check his lengthy article *I Was a Ufologist For the CIA*, published in *UFO magazine*, Vol. 8, No. 6, 1993, where he gives a detailed chronology of his official career, saying that in fact his ufological interests were entirely private.

Because his monograph *Roswell in Perspective* had not come out as of this writing (though it should be available by the time you read this column), we decided to track him down and get his opinions and a summary of what he calls "an interim report" on Roswell.

Pflock stated in an exclusive interview that "essentially what I am attempting to do in the report is to really put things into perspective, really get down solidly what it is we really know about Roswell as opposed to what we think we know about Roswell." He examined both the so-called "conventional wisdom" and "the revisionist view of Roswell, the new scenario with the July 4 crash and the impact site just north of Roswell and so on."

Although Pflock said he didn't intentionally want to criticize R&S, he made no bones about his skepticism on the quality of their research. "I frankly think that the case for the new scenario is extremely weak, that it appears to depend almost in its entirety on the testimony of two witnesses who I find highly questionable."

Pflock gave us a number of reasons why he thinks the testimony of these two key witnesses—Ragsdale and MacKenzie whom he identified as one Frank J. Kaufmann, who also appears in the book under his real name as a more peripheral player—was suspect. A thorough examination of their pitfalls would take too much space, but if Pflock is correct, that would explain why R&S were so vague in providing background on these characters and would not even cooperate in the Congressman's official efforts.

Another weakness in the R&S scenario concerns what Pflock calls "the fizzle in the sky" nighttime sightings that somewhat corroborate the July 4 date and crash site. Basically, R&S combine three different sightings—one by Franciscan Catholic nuns in Roswell, another by Corporal Pyles who was stationed at the base, and a third by rancher William Woody and his father—to make their case for an unusual phenomenon on the night of July 4.

According to Pflock, however, the witnesses' testimonies have been stretched by R&S to fit their scenario: "They represent it though each of these sightings have enough things in common, important things like the trajectory and the direction in which they were seen and so forth, such that you can say that they were all seeing the same thing, and it was all on the 4th and it was the object falling out of the sky. It's just not there, none of them suggest anything more than an astronomical event of some kind."

Pflock interviewed both Pyles and Woody and says the first could not remember at all the date, while the latter signed an affidavit stating he and his father were at their farm where "they saw an incredible bright object appearing on the southwestern quadrant of the sky following an almost due-north track."

Because Woody's farm was south of Roswell and the impact site was north of the city, R&S have to position the sighting as coming out of a northwestern quadrant and following a southeasterly track.

Not All the Findings Were Negative

Pflock emphasized in our interview that not all his findings were negative. He is particularly impressed with the testimony of the mortician Glenn Dennis, saying he "started off as a total skeptic about his story" but now "I've really gotten to know a lot about Glenn Dennis and I am firmly convinced that he is telling the truth as he believes it."

Pflock explained that, "we're beginning to get some back-up to Glenn's story," including a former technician in the base hospital laboratory who remembers the nurse who told Dennis about the alien bodies, and "a fellow who is now on the Roswell City Council, a former police chief who at the time of the event was a motorcycle cop."

Strange Phone Calls from the Base

Pflock explained that the Ballard Funeral Home where Dennis worked had a little coffee shop where cops used to stop for free coffee. This man "remembers very well Glenn telling him about getting these strange phone calls from the base," the mysterious calls which asked Dennis about embalming procedures and whether the funeral home had child-size coffins.

Pflock also told us that Dennis now remembers the exact date when he met the nurse at the Officer's Club, which coincided with the headline in the *Roswell Daily Record* about the capture of a flying saucer. "He says there is no doubt that it was that afternoon after he met with the nurse that he saw that story," said Pflock.

That puts it precisely on July 8 and his confrontation with the military at the hospital on the previous day, all of which should cause some havoc not only on the R&S timeline, but on the the previous ones as well. Pflock summed up his "interim report" by saying that "I think what we've got after you strip away all of the speculation and all of the misinformation and so forth is still an extremely important case…we've got something very unusual on our hands, but beyond that I don't know what else we can say at this point. There are several scenarios you can construct."

He added that an important point he made in his report is that "you don't have to explain everything that has been told about this case by some grand theory that works it all in." In other words, the final explanation for the Roswell mystery may involve a combination of things.

Pflock also gave us an update on the GAO investigation. "The GAO is constrained by its methodology and its charter to do things in particular ways," he said.

"So that what they are doing is a study of the Air Force—not just the Air Force but the Department of Defense, military departments, CIA, everybody involved—about the procedures and methodologies followed in documenting and handling that documentation of air crashes, balloon crashes, anomalous air vehicles crashes, everything across the spectrum, including specifically this event which took place near Roswell."

Air Force Investigation

The search itself has not been conducted by the GAO but by the services themselves. The Air Force has already "something like 25 reserve officers who work in the classification review specifically doing archival research to find documents associated with Roswell." Furthermore, continued Pflock, Congressman Schiff "has given them [the GAO] very explicit instructions, he wants best not fast, he wants to be sure that they come back with real answers that are solidly documented."

UFO Chronicle
J. Antonio Huneeus
January 1995

The Empire Strikes Back— The USAF Roswell Report

THE LONG-HELD AIR FORCE SILENCE with regard to the famous UFO crash near Roswell, New Mexico, in July 1947 has been construed by many ufologists as evidence of the government's cover-up in the affair. For 14 years—since the so-called Roswell incident was revived in 1980 with a book—the USAF didn't revise or comment upon their last act in the Roswell drama: General Ramey's now famous press conference in Fort Worth, Texas, debunking the mysterious debris as a mundane weather balloon.

It was, in fact, the Pentagon's own lack of adequate responsiveness to a query from New Mexico Republican Congressman Steven Schiff, as chronicled in my June 1994 column, that triggered the government's first official inquiry into Roswell. Unsatisfied with what he considered stonewalling,

Schiff requested a probe by the General Accounting Office (GAO). This initiated an official audit last January entitled *Records Management Procedures Dealing With Weather Balloon, Unknown Aircraft, and Similar Crash Incidents,* with Roswell as the main showcase. The Air Force was now legally obliged to respond, and it quickly did so.

In July, USAF Col. Richard L. Weaver, who is Director of the Security and Special Program Oversight (SAF/AAZ), signed a 23-page *Report of Air Force Research Regarding the "Roswell Incident,"* prepared for the GAO. The USAF also released several hundred pages of attachments consisting of some GAO-related memoranda, sworn statements, and transcripts of interviews with retired military personnel and scientists. Also included were documents and technical reports dealing with Project Mogul, a once highly classified effort to detect Soviet nuclear explosions by using sophisticated microphones placed on balloons, now blamed by many for the Roswell debris found in the summer of 1947.

"It is recommended that this document serve as the final Air Force report related to the Roswell matter, for the GAO, or any other inquiries," stated the report's last sentence.

Last September, Secretary of the Air Force Sheila Widnall ordered the public release of the report. Although it did make front page in *The New York Times* and *USA Today* and was reported by the Associated Press, the story was quickly forgotten by the media. Leading Roswell researchers Stanton Friedman and Kevin Randle denounced it on a Larry King UFO Special broadcast from Rachel, Nevada, October 1 on TNT. Friedman and Randle have waged a long and bitter feud over aspects of the Roswell incident, but none of it emerged during the King show. Randle said the Air Force had reinvented the balloon cover story with Mogul, while Friedman maintained that "the Air Force attempted to stage a preemptive strike against the GAO."

Many other ufologists and UFO buffs with whom I've talked to or seen at recent conferences totally rejected the report without even bothering to find out what kind of evidence the USAF had.

"Final Official Air force Response"

In the executive summary and introduction sections, Colonel Weaver provides a history of how the SAF/AAZ became officially involved in support of the GAO. He adds that the report was intended to stand as the final official Air Force statement regarding the matter.

Weaver gives a short account of how the incident "was originally reported in 1947" and how the story evolved through books and TV programs "From the rather benign description of the 'event' and the recovery of some material as described in the original newspaper accounts," writes Weaver, "the 'Roswell Incident' has since grown to mythical (if not mystical) proportions in the eyes and minds of some researchers, portions of the media, and at least part of the American public." Weaver then notes that "these claims are further complicated by the fact that UFO researchers are not in agreement among themselves as to exactly where these recovery sites were located or even the dates of the alleged crash(es)."

Weaver admits there is some measure of credibility to the claims and that some of the authors have an apparent depth of research, but he notes that "what is uniquely lacking...is official positive documentary or physical evidence of any kind that supports the claims of those who allege that something unusual happened."

A few researchers like Friedman believe such documentary evidence exists in the form of the Majestic 12 briefing paper, which the same Colonel Weaver declared fraudulent prior to his Roswell involvement. In the section entitled "Search Strategy and Methodology," Weaver reports that popular UFO literature on the case was reviewed, witnesses were interviewed, and records were searched in various USAF historical and intelligence archives, including "records of the highest classification and compartmentation," such as Special Access Programs (SAPs). The report states that "if the Air Force had recovered some type of extraterrestrial spacecraft and/or bodies and was exploiting this for scientific and technological purposes, then such a program would be operated as a SAP." He adds SAF/AAZ categorically stated that no such Special Access Program(s) exists that pertains to extraterrestrial spacecraft/aliens.

The report goes on to explain that an "SAF/AAZD Declassification Review Team" with authority to "declassify any classified record they found that might be related to Roswell" conducted record searches at dozens of military and government institutions. In the section "What the Roswell Incident Was Not," the USAF report lists and dismisses "an airplane crash, a missile crash, a nuclear accident, and an extraterrestrial craft."

We are told that "the researchers found no indication of heightened activity anywhere else in the military hierarchy in the July 1947 message traffic or orders (to include classified traffic)," which would have been the case if an unknown alien spacecraft had crashed near Roswell.

In the "What the 'Roswell Incident' Was" section, the report finally gets to its main point. It marshalls all the evidence available in the public record pointing to a downed balloon. It cites the photographs showing debris from a balloon and a Rawin target taken during General Ramey's press conference. To the USAF, this was the actual debris and not the substitute cover story and materials proposed by ufologists.

Likewise, the report quotes several witnesses' affidavits collected by the Fund for UFO Research, which support a balloon explanation. For instance, Bessie Brazel Schrieber, daughter of rancher W. W. Brazel who found the wreckage at the Foster Ranch, writes "...the debris looked like pieces of a large balloon which had burst...Sticks, like kite sticks, were attached to some of the pieces with a whitish tape. The tape was about two or three inches wide and had flower-like designs on it." That doesn't sound like pieces from an advanced alien society.

Cavitt's Testimony

Critics of the report will no doubt point out that the SAF/AAZ team was extremely selective in their quotes from witnesses. That is true, but the same can be said of the pro-Roswell books and programs, where quotes about the alleged unusual characteristics of the material are always highlighted.

Just as the pro-Roswell camp had Major Marcel as its star witness, the USAF had theirs in Lt. Col. (Ret.) Sheridan Cavitt, whom they call "the only living eyewitness to the actual debris field and the material found." Cavitt was always the shadowy figure in the Roswell books, who accompanied Major Marcel and Brazel to the Corona field, and would not talk about it later because of a national security oath.

The story is quite different according to Cavitt. He tells his side with full details and many disparaging comments about various ufologists he has dealt with over the years. He told them the whole truth long ago, he says, but they didn't want to hear it and have often misquoted him. Yes, he did go to the field with his subordinate Bill Rickett, and possibly with Jesse Marcel, although he doesn't remember Brazel.

In his sworn statement, Cavitt writes that "when we got to this location, we subsequently located some debris which appeared to me to resemble bamboo-type square sticks one-quarter to one-half-inch square that were very light, as well as some sort of metallic reflecting material that was also very light…The area of this debris was very small, about 20 feet square, and the material was spread on the ground, but there was no gouge or crater or other obvious sign of impact. I remember recognizing this material as being consistent with a weather balloon." He later repeats in the statement that "I thought at the time and think so now, that this debris was from a crashed balloon."

In the 30-page transcript of his interview with Colonel Weaver, Cavitt elaborates further on each of his main points. The photos of the debris in General Ramey's office are definitely consistent with what he saw in the field; he wrote no classified report about the expedition because he thought it was a waste of time and effort. He liked Jesse Marcel and Bill Rickett and knew them well. He "considered them to be good men, however, both did tend to exaggerate things on occasion."

Finally, Cavitt states "I am not part of any conspiracy to withhold information from anyone, either the U.S. Government or the American public. I have never been sworn to any form of secrecy by anyone concerning this matter." He makes several other statements reiterating that he has not been threatened or coerced by the government. "My bottom line," he concludes, "is that this whole incident was no big deal and it certainly did not involve anything extraterrestrial."

Although he admits his memory may be faltering on specific details and it had to be often refreshed by his wife Mary during the interview, Cavitt is so sure and definite in the main thrust of his account about what transpired near Roswell back in 1947 that the only way the pro-Roswell camp will be able to rationalize it is to accuse him of perpetuating the cover-up, precisely what he denies doing.

The rest of the report—actually the bulk of it—is the Air Force attempt to explain the Roswell debris in terms of one of many tests of balloon clusters with radar targets and acoustical equipment, undertaken by New York University for Project Mogul at the Alamogordo Army Air Field (later Holloman Air Force Base) in New Mexico.

USAF investigators located and interviewed Athelstan Spilhaus, Director of the NYU Balloon Project, Col. Albert Trakowski, the USAF project officer, and project engineer Charles B. Moore. Spilhaus had never even heard of Roswell prior to the interview, and Trakowski could only provide general background on the project and only one specific tidbit, a phone call from a close associate at Wright Field.

"He just wanted to let me know that someone had come to him with some debris from New Mexico, and he said, 'this sure looked like some of the stuff that you launched from Alamogordo,'" wrote Trakowski in his statement.

Of all the Mogul personnel, C. B. Moore, a renowned expert on balloons now with the Langmuir Laboratory for Atmospheric Research in Socorro, New Mexico, had far more to say about the Mogul tests and their link to Roswell. In a 54-page transcript of an interview with two USAF officers, Moore explained everything you ever wanted to know about balloon testing in the late 1940s. The scientific and military details about Project Mogul, "that we might be able to detect nuclear blasts via pressure waves and low frequency microphones" stationed in constant-level balloons, are fascinating but beyond this column's scope.

While Moore was the man in charge of all balloon testing for the project, carried on under an ad hoc cover of atmospheric research, he was not aware of the name Mogul until 1992, when he was contacted by an independent researcher. In his sworn statement, C. B. Moore concludes that "I can think of no other explanation for Roswell than one of our early June service flight balloons… This flight was with multiple balloons and targets and may have had a sonobuoy [black box?]."

Moore also provided a plausible explanation for the hieroglyphs described by Major Marcel and his son. The reflector material used a tape reinforcement with flowers and geometric figures made by "a toy or novelty company" in New York.

Based on Moore's testimony, a contemporary diary of one of the scientists, and other data, Colonel Weaver writes that "Flight 4 was launched on June 4, 1947, but was not recovered by the NYU group. It is very probable that this Top Secret project balloon train [Flight 4], made up of unclassified components, came to rest some miles northwest of Roswell, New Mexico, became shredded in the surface winds, and was ultimately found by the rancher, Brazel, ten days later."

Why there was so much fuss over a decayed neoprene balloon and its wooden and metallic components, which captivated Major Marcel and led to a press announcement of a disc recovered by the Roswell base and flights with the material to Fort Worth and Wright Field, is not satisfactorily explained in the USAF report. Concerning Lieutenant Haut's now famous press release with all its ensuing confusion, Colonel Weaver points out accurately that in early July, 1947, "nobody for sure knew" what the terms flying saucer or flying disc meant, "since they had only been in use for a couple of weeks."

While this report may be the USAF's final official word on the matter as intended, it surely won't stop the Roswell legend and its proponents in the UFO community, the city itself with its fledgling museums, and the media. It is too late for that.

It should be added, however, that Mogul has subscribers within the ufological community. In fact, it was Robert Todd, a researcher best known for his persistent efforts to obtain government documents under the Freedom of Information Act, who first proposed a Mogul test for Roswell back in 1990. Todd is credited by Weaver as having an "almost encyclopedic knowledge of the complexities of Air Force records systems."

Similarly, Karl Pflock, in his recent interim report *Roswell in Perspective,* published by the Fund for UFO Research, also endorses Mogul as the most logical explanation for the debris field. Pflock, however, believes there was a second incident with recovered bodies—the source of mortician Glenn Dennis' famous testimony—which remains to be explained and could, in his opinion, involve aliens.

It was my aim to review the USAF report in a civilized manner without antagonism or finger pointing so readers can see for themselves what the Pentagon has to say. It is my guess that when the GAO finishes and releases its own report in the near future, it will probably confirm the conclusions of the Air Force, thus burying any hope of political progress with regard to the issue of Roswell. But the crash and recovery of an alien spacecraft and little gray men in the New Mexico desert will live on as a legend.

UFO Chronicle
J. Antonio Huneeus
July 1996

Roswell is once again in the news, thanks to a recent incident that's focusing world attention on the famous case.

New Metallic Artifact

A VISITOR WALKED into the International UFO Museum and Research Center in downtown Roswell, New Mexico, on March 24, 1996. He told museum Secretary Treasurer Max Littell that he had a metallic fragment recovered from the famous July 1947 UFO crash by a mysterious soldier. Littell had heard many similar claims. "I'd be happy to take a look at the piece if you can bring it in," he told the out-of-state visitor. Twenty minutes later he was presented with a small metal fragment of triangular shape mounted on a flat glass frame.

Within days the story was in the Roswell papers and all over the world. Had definitive proof of the 1947 alien craft finally been produced? Don't hold your breath. Thanks to James Moseley, editor of the UFO newsletter *Saucer Smear*, and other sources, we obtained several reports about the fragment. The most complete one was written by Miller Johnson, an industrial designer who created a display of the Project MOGUL/New York University secret balloon tests (the now official USAF version of the event) at the International UFO Museum. We also have the preliminary report by C. B. "Charlie" Moore, a senior professor at the School of Mines in Socorro, New Mexico, who was present during the fragment's X-ray fluorescence analysis.

The potential value of the piece to Roswell was illustrated by the fact that the city's chief of police, Ray Mounts, guarded the fragment during the 90-mile drive between the museum and the New Mexico Bureau of Mines and Mineral Resources in Socorro, where the tests were conducted. Johnson, who was also present, described the piece when it was taken out of its frame and photographed: "The fragment had parallel creases that extended from one end to the other, with a gaping hole at its center. The back side has a high-gloss silvery look with no copper showing. The silvery colored surfaces were void of any tarnish." The three roughly triangular sides measured 80 millimeters, 78 millimeters, and 43 millimeters, with a 29-millimeter hole in the center of the fragment.

The X-ray fluorescence analysis conducted by Chris McKee of the Bureau of Mines determined, according to Johnson's report, that "the front side analysis indicated that it was about 50 percent Cu [copper] and about 50 percent Ag [silver]. The back side analysis showed about 87 percent Ag, 12 percent Cu and 1 percent trace elements. The fragment weighed in at 16.160 grams." So far everybody agrees that the fragment appears to have a terrestrial rather than an ET origin. Here is an excerpt of Charlie Moore's report: "The fragment clearly was not related to one of the radar targets or any of the other equipment used by the NYU group. Such a diaphragm may have been in the microphone section of the sonobuoys that we flew, but, if this were the case, there is the question as to how it became exposed so that the alleged GI could have pocketed it." Moore was the manager of the NYU balloon cluster tests at Alamogordo in 1947 for top secret Project MOGUL.

More germane to the original Roswell debris story is the following comment from Moore's report: "The fragment could have been bent easily; it could have been dented with a sledge hammer if one hit it. It clearly had been torn from its original setting. There was nothing associated with it to suggest an exotic nature or an exotic origin; it appeared to me to be a component of some terrestrial, technical artifact." Moore has also enthusiastically backed an idea proposed by David Thomas of the non-profit group New Mexicans for Science and Reason. It consists of isotopic analysis to see, as Moore summarized it, "if the copper in the fragment has a different isotopic composition than that of terrestrial copper."

Thomas explained that "the earthly ratios for the common isotopes of copper are 69.09 percent (Cu-63) and 30.91 percent (Cu-65). These would probably be different for Cu not from our own solar system." The isotopic test has not yet been initiated since a small portion of the sample must first be "vaporized and ionized in a vacuum." However, permission from the owner must be obtained before destroying the tiny sample. Meanwhile, we heard reports that yet another alleged metallic piece was acquired by the Space & UFO Museum in Hakui City, Japan, which will open officially next July. Stay tuned for results, if any.

Latest Official Reports

In October 1995, the USAF released a thick volume of over 1,000 pages, *The Roswell Report—Fact vs. Fiction in the New Mexico Desert*. It includes Col. Richard Weaver's original 1994 *Report of Air Force Research Regarding the Roswell Incident*, with all its attachments, and a new short Introduction by Lt. James McAndrew. Among the attachments are sworn statements and transcripts of interviews with retired military personnel and scientists, and lengthy, technical declassified reports on Project MOGUL. A photo section of balloon tests and air force personnel is also included. After years of accusing the USAF of remaining silent about Roswell, the UFO community has curiously ignored the release of this report.

The U.S. Congress General Accounting Office (GAO), meanwhile, released its own thin, 20-page report to New Mexico Rep. Steven Schiff—*Government Records: Results of a Search for Records Concerning the 1947 Crash Near Roswell, New Mexico*—in July 1995. The search conducted by Richard Davis, director of the GAO National Security Analysis, came up practically empty-handed. The CIA, FBI, Department of Energy, and other agencies were queried for documents that may explain the Roswell crash, but their response was always that "no such documents" were found. The GAO did determine that the "RAAF [Roswell Army Air Field] administrative records (from October 1945 through December 1949) and RAAF outgoing messages (from October 1946 through December 1949) were destroyed."

Roswell proponents have made much of the fact that the RAAF destroyed documents for the 1945–49 period. Government agencies routinely destroy large numbers of documents. In my opinion, so far, absence of evidence—in this case, lack of official documentation to prove the alien nature of the Roswell crash—cannot be construed as positive evidence. While Congressman Schiff has apparently dropped the matter, the USAF has one more report in the wings, with further negative findings.

Other research with government documents obtained through the Freedom of Information Act (FOIA) has produced what could be construed as a "negative paper trail" for Roswell. One of the latest documents obtained is the transcript of the "Scientific Advisory Board Conference" held at the Pentagon on March 17–18, 1948, which was attended by the USAF's top scientific consultants. The meeting was presided over by Gen. Hoyt Vandenberg (of MJ-12 fame). The scientific chairman was Dr. Theodore von Karman. A number of sensitive USAF projects were discussed during the two-day conference.

Out of nearly 300 pages of minutes from the various secret briefings, only one paragraph is devoted to UFOs. Col. Howard McCoy was discussing the "Utilization of Technical Intelligence" when he mentioned a newly-created USAF probe. He said, "We have a new project—Project SIGN—which may surprise you as a development from the so-called mass hysteria of the past summer when we had all the unidentified flying objects or discs. This can't be laughed off. We have over 300 reports which haven't been publicized in the papers from very competent personnel… and practically all Air Force [and] airline people with broad experience. We are running down every report."

So far so good, but the bad news for Roswell proponents came in Colonel McCoy's last phrase: "I can't even tell you how much we would give to have one of those crash in an area so that we could recover whatever they are." Bear in mind that it took almost 50 years to declassify this document and that its release was not willingly volunteered by the USAF. Despite the total lack of a paper trail about Roswell, the saucer blues in this small New Mexico town continue to be bigger than ever.

UFO Chronicle
July 1997

Special Guest Columnist: James E. McWilliams

FOR 50 YEARS, ufologists have been fascinated by the mystery that started at 9:50 p.m. on July 2, 1947, in Roswell, New Mexico.

That's when the Wilmot family first reported a "big glowing object... like two inverted saucers faced mouth-to-mouth." They said the object shot across the sky from the southeast to the northwest.

During an electrical storm that evening, W. W. "Mac" Brazel and two of his children heard something like an explosion. He assumed it had been thunder—until the next day when Mac found unusual wreckage scattered over a quarter-mile-long stretch of his land. Six days later, Lt. Walter Haut at the Roswell Army Air Base informed the press that base intelligence officer Maj. Jesse A. Marcel had picked up the remains of a flying disk that had crashed at an area ranch. The news received international publicity.

The military quickly recanted, saying the debris recovered at Roswell came from a weather device. Over the years, Marcel and other eyewitnesses have claimed otherwise. Numerous books and articles have attempted to shed light on the subject, but the best way to learn about the alleged UFO cover-up is to go there yourself.

Here's a quick guide to five must-see spots in Roswell:

International UFO Museum

Deon Crosby has the right qualifications for her new job as the director of the International UFO Museum and Research Center in Roswell: She has actually seen UFOs.

"I was driving toward Roswell from Vaughn between 10 p.m. and midnight," she said, "when I saw four rotating lights toward the Roswell horizon. They rotated around me in a peculiar pattern and motion. I saw something that I was unable to identify."

Crosby, who became the museum's director in May 1996, places great credence in the findings of researchers such as Stanton Friedman, Leonard Stringfield, and Linda Moulton Howe. "The strongest evidence, I believe," she said, "is the personal witness of the people I know to be credible."

The museum opened on September 27, 1991, with the collaboration of Walter Haut, Glenn Dennis, and Max Littell. Haut was the public relations officer who wrote and released the Roswell incident story. Dennis was the mortician who became involved in the incident at the base hospital, and Max Littell was the business partner who helped crystallize the venture. The museum is located in the Plains Theater at 114 North Main in Roswell. Opposition to the museum has been prominent in some quarters. "In the '60s, the mayor of this town basically mandated that nothing related to UFOs would be connected to Roswell," Deon said. "He didn't want Roswell to become, as he called it, 'kook city.'"

Today, the museum is recognized and supported by the current mayor and local residents. In 1996, the Tourism Association of New Mexico presented the museum with the Top Tourist Destination of New Mexico Award. The new museum boasts exhibits covering all aspects of the 1947 Roswell incident plus other exhibits on space, crop circles, abductions, cattle mutilations, and ancient cultures.

The North Impact Site

About 30 miles north of Roswell on Highway 285, a sign marks a turn to the west. If you travel about eight miles west from the turnoff, you will find the North Impact Site, also known as the Kaufman Site.

Herbert Miller "Hub" Corn is the proud owner of this piece of UFO history, something he discovered when he took over the family farm. He noticed people driving around on his land and wondered what they were doing. Finally, he asked a state police officer and learned that they were searching for the site where a UFO came down in July 1947.

People sometimes take property from the site without his permission, Hub said. "A guy called the museum three or four months ago trying to sell them dirt from the impact site. I told them to get his number so I could see where my real estate was going."

Hub will take visitors to the site for a $15 fee, because he says the tours cut into his principal livelihood, ranching and farming. People come from all 50 states and several foreign countries to visit the site. Even celebrities come for the tour. "We had Jonathan Frakes [star of *Star Trek: The Next Generation*], some of David Letterman's crew, and an assortment of writers and songwriters," he recalled.

Hub gives visitors an information sheet titled "On the Roswell Crash Impact Site." Written by noted UFO author Kevin Randle, it explains why Hub's property is considered the site of the famous UFO impact. Many people—including Frank Kaufman and Major Edwin Easley—claim to have seen the crashed UFO on Hub's property.

The West Impact Site

Less well known than the North Site, the West Site surfaced in 1993 when Max Littell of the International UFO Museum and Research Center in Roswell visited James Ragsdale at the request of an author. Ragsdale told of a UFO crash in the nearby Lincoln National Forest that he and a friend had witnessed. Five days before his death on July 1, 1995, he signed an affidavit to set the record straight.

He said that he and a female friend were camped off Arabella Road near Boy Scout Mountain (about 53 miles west of Roswell) on Friday, July 4, 1947. At about 11:30 p.m., they saw a flash, and then a flaming craft came toward them from the north. It crashed within 60 yards of their truck.

Examination of the crash that night and the next morning revealed a saucer-shaped craft about 20 feet in diameter with a dome in the middle. The craft had struck two large boulders and split open near the bottom.

Ragsdale described the four dead bodies inside as strange-looking "little people" less than four feet tall. The craft's interior, he said, was fascinating—both in its workmanship and in its beauty.

Ragsdale's story has caused some researchers to postulate that two extraterrestrial craft collided near Corona, New Mexico. One craft, saucer-shaped, crashed near Boy Scout Mountain west of Roswell. The other, a bat-shaped craft, crashed north of Roswell. While eyewitness testimony at the North Site is well documented, researchers hope other witnesses will be able to corroborate Ragsdale's story.

Directions to the West Impact Site can be picked up at the International UFO Museum and Research Center.

Hangar 84

Anyone paying a visit to Roswell should be sure to see Hangar 84 off of east Enterprise Street in the Roswell Industrial Air Park. The park is in southern Roswell and was formerly Roswell Army Air Field, later named Walker Air Force Base. One can view the hangar's exterior without permission, but to go inside requires permission from Renown Aviation.

Back in 1947, this hangar was known as hangar P-3 and was reputed to have been the temporary storage site of UFO wreckage and alien bodies. Witnesses stated that the bodies were packed in dry ice and stored in a large crate placed in the middle of the empty hangar. Military police surrounded the perimeter, both inside and outside the building, to ensure security.

Supposedly, on Monday, July 7, 1947, at 2:00 a.m., under the cover of darkness, the bodies and materials were secretly loaded onto two separate aircraft. One of them headed for Fort Worth Army Air Field. From there, the cargo was taken to other military installations for inspection by high-ranking military and civilian authorities.

One witness, Frank Kaufman, reported that the bodies were flown out in two separate flights to guard against all of them being lost in one accident. The second aircraft was routed directly to Wright Army Air Field.

Hangar 84 is the famous hangar where Oliver Wendell "Pappy" Henderson allegedly viewed the UFO wreckage and bodies before flying them on to their individual destinations and places in UFO history.

The Enigma UFO Museum

In 1987, John Arnold Price and his wife Sherron opened the Outa' Limits Video Store. Since Price was interested in the Roswell UFO incident, he decided to put some displays in his store window concerning MJ-12, the 1952 document that purportedly informed President Eisenhower that the U.S. government had recovered two crashed UFOs and established the secret "Majestic-12" group to deal with "extraterrestrial biological entities."

The store became a hot spot for UFO researchers and Roswell witnesses. Price's own interest deepened; and he researched the phenomenon further, adding new displays to the store.

In 1990, UFO skeptic Phil Klass debated Clifford Stone, a local UFO researcher at the store. Store traffic was heavy that night and interfered with the videotaping of the debate. Later, when the problem repeated itself during an interview of Glenn Dennis, the mortician involved with the Roswell incident, Price decided to separate the UFO displays and video store. So, in April 1992, he officially opened the UFO Enigma Museum.

The Roswell crash scene in the Blue Room is one if visitors' favorite displays. It depicts a crashed saucer with three dead aliens and one live one in the custody of an army M.P Other displays feature photos and artifacts of UFOs, both stateside and overseas.

Researchers and authors Kevin Randle, Donald Schmitt, and Stanton Friedman have visited the museum. Celebrities and politicians have also dropped in, but Price says the latter keep a low profile.

Roswell UFO Bombshell
Was the crashed spaceship really a lost A-bomb?

Jim Keith
January 2000

My source on the following story has asked me to be very vague in my description of him. He describes himself as "a longtime researcher/ instructor of engineering at a school in New Mexico." I know specific details of his professional work, as well as the names of his own sources for the following information, but he has asked me not to mention them because of potential problems involving security clearances. Speaking with me recently, he told me about his knowledge of what actually took place in Roswell, New Mexico, in July 1947—an event which has been alleged by many researchers to have been the crash of an alien spacecraft. His information is gleaned from conversations with others in the engineering field and in the military who were living in or near Roswell at the time. I realize that without identifying my source, the following information is rendered suspect; with that in mind it may still open up new areas of research that will crack the Roswell case. Here is the gist of what he told me:

World War II was over, and America had a secret to conceal. Although the government said there were 500 atomic bombs in the military's arsenal, that was a lie. There were none that were considered reliable. Due to a number of factors—corrosion of parts kept in storage, batteries that didn't work, faulty initiators, and other reasons—there were no usable nuclear bombs in American military stockpiles. After the end of the war, the operational team in charge of the nuclear arsenal had also been dispersed, many of them going to other jobs, and some leaving the military altogether. In short, there was no real nuclear deterrent against the Soviet threat, and members of the American government and military who realized this were terrified that the Soviets would find out.

The American brass sought to remedy the situation. As part of this fix, testing of nuclear delivery systems was moved during 1945 and 1946 from Wendover, Utah, to the 509th U.S. Army Air Force Bomb Group unit in Roswell, New Mexico. At the time, Roswell was the center of much secret testing, including the top secret balloon program Project Mogul, and "non-critical" testing at the Trinity blast site. One job that was given to the 509th was the operational testing of nuclear bombs, including fine-tuning the ability to hit targets accurately.

Another secret: According to my source, military bombers were notoriously unreliable in hitting targets, sometimes missing their mark by as much as half a mile. It was given to the 509th to improve that record, and to make it possible to deliver bombs, particularly nuclear bombs, with greater accuracy. "Live" as well as "dummy" bombs were flown in from Sandia to Roswell, where they were tested and used in target drops.

It was in this environment that the most famous of all UFO stories was born. According to my source, the true story behind the alleged UFO crash was that there was an accident involving a B-29 flying from the Army Air Force Base in Sandia (Albuquerque) to Roswell. From the statements of men in the military who were there at the time, my source states that either an atomic bomb or what is termed a "bomb shape," or "test shape," the shell of a nuke lacking explosives and atomic capability, and sometimes filled with concrete to add weight, was accidentally or purposefully jettisoned above Corona, New Mexico, directly on the flight path between Sandia and Roswell. Along with the bomb, metal foil used for radar jamming, termed "chaff," may have also been dropped.

The accidental dropping of a nuclear weapon would surely have been cause enough for a cover-up. If this information had leaked to the public, there might have been an extremely negative reaction.

As an aside, my source mentioned that either an armed atomic bomb or "test shape," flattened by impact with the ground, could have looked like a squashed disk.

Maintenance reports on the 509th show that B-29s accidentally releasing their payload was not an uncommon occurrence. My source tells me that an atomic bomb was accidentally dropped several hundred yards past the runway at Sandia, near the present location of Gibson Avenue, in about 1954. The high explosives used for setting off the bomb detonated on impact, leaving a crater that remains to this day, but the atomic unit did not detonate. A year later another nuclear bomb was dropped by the military off Vancouver Island. [Editor's note: Such accidents were not limited to the 1940s and '50s. At the U.S. government's National Atomic Museum in Albuquerque, New Mexico, a display tells of an incident in 1966 in which four nuclear bombs were dropped on the coast of Spain following the collision of two U.S. Air Force planes. One of the bombs was missing for almost three months. See *www.atomicmuseum.com* for details.]

It may not be possible to verify the flight from Sandia to Roswell, since crews taking this route sometimes did not bother with flight plans.

Jesse Marcel, the 509th Group's intelligence officer who claimed to have handled parts from an alien craft, may have been set up as a patsy. People who worked with Marcel characterized him as being an essentially overzealous security guard, and not well liked. My source believes that there may have been persons who wanted to get back at Marcel, and perhaps make him look foolish by convincing him that he had seen a "flying saucer."

What of the alien bodies that some witnesses have said were found in or near the wreckage? Some, if not all, of these reports have been discredited, or at least rendered suspect in recent years—they may exist only as an imaginative gloss on what actually took place. Certainly the majority of such reports tend to fall apart on close inspection.

My source says he was in touch with an astrophysicist (whom he has named to me) who defected from Russia in the 1960s. The Russian claimed that he had been part of the Soviet equivalent to America's Project Blue Book. He said that the Russians were very interested in the Roswell incident. After the story was released to the news media, Russian agents in the United States were ordered to find out what really happened. The Russians did not believe the "flying saucer" story; in fact, they were quite sure that the Americans were using this tale as a cover for something involving military technology.

The Russians may have been right. The Roswell UFO-crash story may have been the U.S. military's desperate attempt to obscure a nightmarish blunder—the accidental release of an atomic bomb over New Mexico.

Frank Kaufmann: Roswell Eyewitness?

Kevin D. Randle
December 2001

FRANK KAUFMANN, one of the most controversial of the Roswell UFO crash figures, died in February 2001, leaving many questions unanswered. If what he said was true, then any explanation for the Roswell UFO crash, other than the extraterrestrial, vanishes. His firsthand observations of the craft, of the bodies, and of the extraordinary efforts by the military to hide the facts leaves no other explanation. That is, of course, if he was telling us the truth.

Kaufmann was originally from New York and had studied art there before the Second World War dragged him to New Mexico. He was an accomplished artist, and his many paintings hung throughout his house. They

Frank J. Kaufmann (1916–2001).

ranged from landscapes to still life to a few portraits. To my admittedly unskilled eye, they reflected a very talented man.

Kaufmann's Military Career

During World War II, Kaufmann served in the Army Air Force as an enlisted man. He rose to master sergeant, according to what he told me, and he never suggested that he had held a commission. He hinted that he was involved in some sort of intelligence work, though this was never fully explained. He talked of Soviet spies coming up through Mexico, of the Norden bombsight that was so important for the war in Europe, and chasing intruders off what was then the Roswell Army Air Field and later Walker Air Force Base.

He mentioned his association with Brig. Gen. Martin F. Scanlon, who did have an association with intelligence work. Prior to the war, Scanlon had been an attaché to the American embassy in London, whose job it was to spy on German attempts to rebuild their air force. Scanlon was called back to the United States, where Hap Arnold, who was commanding the Army Air Force, asked him to help establish what would become, much later, Air Force intelligence.

These links, between Scanlon and intelligence, and between Scanlon and Kaufmann, provided some measure of validity to the things Kaufmann said much later. Kaufmann knew Scanlon, who had served at Roswell, and he was well aware of Scanlon's intelligence work.

After the war, when the size of the military was being reduced, Kaufmann remained in place in Roswell. He was, however, discharged from the Army and apparently hired by the Army as a civilian, doing the same job he had done before his discharge. This, according to the available records, was as a clerk in the personnel office. According to the documents, he left active service on November 7, 1945, and left his civilian job at the base on December 12, 1947. He quit to take a new and, I would assume, a better job in Roswell.

There at the Retrieval

All of this would be unimportant to us if Kaufmann hadn't said that he was involved in the retrieval of an alien craft in July 1947. I learned that he might have something to do with the case from Walter Haut. Although I don't remember the exact words, Haut said that Frank Kaufmann might be a man to talk to.

I called him on January 4, 1990, and conducted what was probably the very first interview that Kaufmann granted. He was, as always, somewhat reluctant to provide information and answered some of the questions with what would eventually become his stock answer when he didn't like a question: "Well, I don't know."

He told me that he had been assigned to the Roswell base in January 1942 and remained there throughout the war. He said, "I was essentially separated in 1945. Then I was frozen for two years. So, I was out there [at the base] as a civilian for two years."

During this interview, Kaufmann first mentioned Robert Thomas, who supposedly knew something about the UFO crash. Kaufmann told me then that Thomas had been a warrant officer. Later, Kaufmann would suggest that Thomas was actually a brigadier general masquerading as a warrant officer because Thomas didn't want to draw attention to himself.

When I asked about a military assignment for Thomas, Kaufmann said, "He had something to do with security...top echelon security. When they took, when they found a lot of this equipment...everything had to be cleared through him first."

Frank Kaufmann at the impact site.

Unsolved Mysteries

Kaufmann and I talked for a few more minutes. Now, reading over the transcript of that first conversation, I can see that I provided hints of what I was looking for, and Kaufmann, sharp as he was, certainly would have picked up on those hints. He also pointed out, as we talked, that he had seen the *Unsolved Mysteries* episode that dealt with the Roswell UFO crash. He also hinted that he had discussed this with Walter Haut. If he needed priming for his story, that certainly would have provided more than enough information.

The hangar where alien bodies remained overnight in 1947, according to Kaufmann.

But there is an interesting note. Kaufmann, talking about the show, said, "There was one thing that came to mind as I watched that program." He then explained that he didn't like the scene in which Jesse Marcel, Sr., after collecting debris on the Brazel (Foster) ranch, returned home with it so he could show it to his wife and son.

I suggested that it wasn't actually classified at that point, but Kaufmann said, "It was classified." That told me something about Kaufmann. At the very least, he understood how these things were supposed to work rather than how civilians believed them to work. Officers did not share classified material with family and friends.

I also pointed out that Marcel had known that the debris was not made on Earth. Kaufmann asked, "How would he know?"

These were a couple of things that bothered Kaufmann. He played the whole thing close to the vest, giving little in the way of information—mainly, I believe, because he didn't know who I was or why I was asking the questions.

Abandoned ranch only 100 yards from road leading to impact site.

That was Frank Kaufmann, however. Hinting that he might know something more than the rest of us, hinting that he was on the inside, but never quite confirming it. I should also point out that in this conversation, Kaufmann told me that he had been an enlisted man and that he had been a civilian employee of the government at the time of the crash. It was only later that some would say that Kaufmann had been an officer, that he had been a colonel in intelligence, but he never mentioned anything like that to me and I don't know where those ideas originated.

I met Frank Kaufmann in person not long after that, on Super Bowl weekend, 1990. We—Don Schmitt and I—visited him at his home in Roswell. We sat in the living room and discussed the case to some extent. He then walked us around, showing us his paintings. They filled the walls of most of the rooms.

The Visit with Kaufmann

There was one painting that he seemed to be very fond of. It was mostly reds and browns, showing large trees late in the year, with a strange, gray-

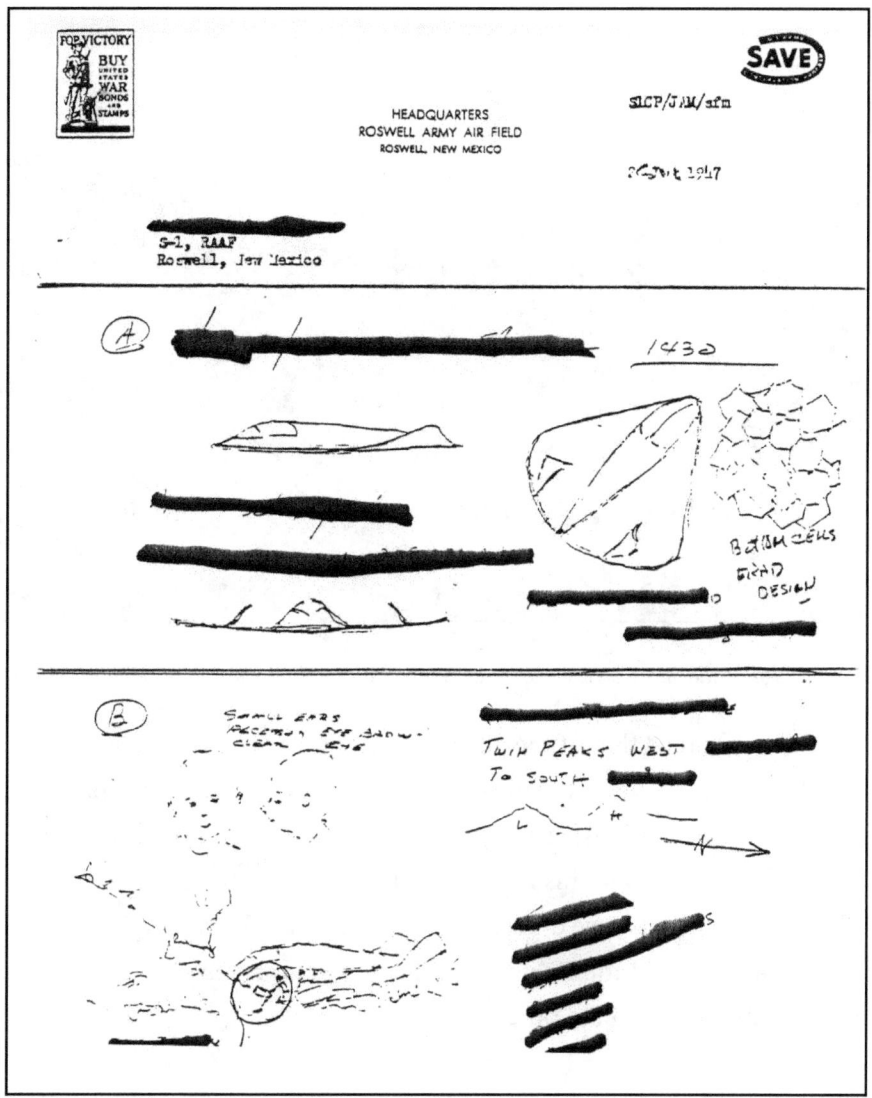

Sketches made by Kaufmann just after the events of July 4, 1947.

ish face superimposed on the trunk of one of the trees. I thought it looked more like an elf than anything extraterrestrial. It was a very strange painting, and I mention it here only because Kaufmann showed us the painting only two weeks after I first spoke to him, but the picture looked as if it had been painted a long time before that. Later, he would hint that

Impact site as identified by Kaufmann; craft found below dip in terrain at center of photo.

the face resembled that of the alien creatures he had seen in July 1947.

After that, whenever I made it into Roswell, I would call Kaufmann and we would go to breakfast, usually to the Roswell Inn. He would slowly provide information about his involvement at these meetings. Finally I asked if we could videotape one of the meetings, and he agreed. We sat in his backyard and discussed the Roswell case, with him on one side of the table and Schmitt and I on the other.

Evolving Story

Kaufmann's story evolved over time. Finally he said that he had been involved from the beginning, that he had been called by Brigadier General Scanlon and asked to drive over to the White Sands Proving Grounds (now the White Sands Missile Range) and see what they had on radar. Kaufmann said that they watched something flit around the sky periodically, but that radar coverage wasn't all that great given both the capabilities of the

Kaufmann with TV documentary crew at impact site.

radar and the mountainous local terrain.

Kaufmann said that they stayed in the radar room for 24 hours, arranging a signal with the operator so that they could go outside or to the latrine. This radar watch, according to Kaufmann, was called off, and he returned to Roswell. Within 24 hours or so, the object was down. Kaufmann said that the radar screen lighted as the craft exploded. Some experts said that a bursting of the craft would not have been reflected on the radar, but there are two ways to explain it. One, when the craft exploded, it sent out a burst of electromagnetic radiation on the same frequency as that used by the radar. The set, reading that burst as a return, would display it in a bright blob of light. Since this was a burst, the signal would fade and the image on the screen would fade. Transponders in commercial airliners can paint the screen in a similar fashion, if the pilot needs to communicate with the controlling radar and flight following center.

Or two, the craft fragmented about the time the maximum signal had been sent so that it painted each of those fragments, displaying them on the screen. It was something that had happened in the past and explains why bombers, attempting to avoid detection, sometimes drop great quantities of "chaff"—they fill the sky with tiny bits of metal, and the radar screen is filled with the blobs of light.

In any case, they knew the craft was down, they had a good idea where it went down, and they were going out to look for it. Given the radar coverage in the area, and given there might not have been ground-based radars in Roswell, it seems hard to believe that they would have known that it was down, or even where it might have crashed.

Kaufmann said that they drove north out of town, turned off on a side road that was little more than a scraped area across the desert, and headed to the west. There was a dull blue glow that pinpointed the location for them.

On the Scene

Once they were on the scene, in a bowl-shaped valley with some kind of strange, triangular-shaped craft impacted in the rocky cliff, they were unsure about how to proceed. The area was checked by a man with a Geiger counter and found to be relatively free of radiation; the others moved forward.

Kaufmann said that the craft was about 15 or 20 feet wide at the widest and shaped like a triangle with rounded edges. The underside had a hexagonal pattern that Kaufmann said he thought might be some kind of power cells.

Outside the craft was a body, sitting next to the cliff, looking as if it had walked over to take a nap. This creature, according to Kaufmann, was about five feet tall, had a head slightly larger than a human head, and eyes that were slightly larger than human eyes. It looked serene, as if at peace with the universe. Kaufmann said that the look on its face, and its seeming peace, always bothered him and was the one thing that stood out over all others.

When they were convinced that there was no danger from radiation, they moved in and examined the area. Kaufmann said that Thomas was in charge, giving orders about the best ways of recovering the craft and the bodies. Kaufmann said that they cleaned the area quickly, taking the bodies to the base first, and then loading the ship onto a truck to be driven to a hangar. The craft was extremely light.

According to Kaufmann, there was a core of nine men commanded by Thomas which included Kaufmann, who had the biggest responsibility for the craft and the bodies. Although Kaufmann hinted that he had been one of the more important of the nine, it would seem that his role was one of the smallest. He simply didn't have the technical expertise, authority, or education for a large role. Instead, he might have been involved simply because he was there and because Scanlon and Thomas knew him and believed they could trust him to keep the secret.

Once the craft and bodies had been removed, experts in camouflage were brought in to hide the signs of the crash. When that had been completed, the military moved off, away from the scene.

Revisiting the Site

Kaufmann, nearly 50 years later, took me to where he claimed the craft had crashed. It was on a ranch now owned by Hub Corn. Back in 1947, the land had belonged to the McKnight family. Near the road that today leads to the crash site is an old, abandoned house, with little to indicate if it had stood there in 1947. Kaufmann said they had passed no house but he seemed to think they had come into the desert farther south.

The International UFO Museum and Research Center in Roswell explored this avenue in the 1990s. They located a McKnight relative, Jim McKnight, and had him sign an affidavit about that aspect of the incident. Although he hadn't lived on the ranch in 1947, he said that he was quite familiar with the area and that all the local residents talked to one another. Had there been a UFO crash on the ranch in 1947, he was sure that he would have heard about it, but he remembered no family discussions of anything concerning UFOs.

McKnight suggested that the only place to cross the Macho River area as you headed west from the highway was near the ranch house. Anyone living there in 1947 would have seen the military as they drove in and out. Again, McKnight claimed that if anything had happened in that area, even though he was a small child in 1947 and didn't live in the area himself, he would have known about it. That he didn't suggested, to him, that nothing had happened, so that Kaufmann's story was in error.

There are, however, some subtle reasons to believe that Kaufmann might have had this inside knowledge. First, he didn't try to convince me that he had been on the debris field, an area about 75 miles northwest of Roswell, and one that was well known by the 1990s. Instead, he showed me a location closer to Roswell, but one that was hidden to the west of Highway 285. To that point, no one had suggested a site that close to the city.

Minor Corroboration

Once he had shown it to me, I began to search for corroboration. One bit of evidence came from an officer I had known for a number of years, who also claimed inside knowledge. After Kaufmann had taken me to the impact site, I asked this officer if he could show me, on a map, where he believed that the object had crashed. I provided no hint that I had seen the location as offered by Kaufmann.

That officer spent 20 minutes going over the maps, cross-checking himself. From discussions we had in the past, I believed he was going to show me a site out west of Roswell, maybe off Highway 380 as it wound its way out toward Riodoso. Instead he pointed at a location north of town within a couple of miles of what Kaufmann had shown me. The officer said, "Without a better map, that's as close as I can get."

Given that he knew nothing about what Kaufmann had told me, and given that I don't believe he or Kaufmann knew one another, it was interesting that he would select, more or less, the same small section of New

Mexico real estate. It was a thin corroboration of what Kaufmann had said, though it was by no means definitive.

In a similar vein, Kaufmann had told me, as he had others, that the crash took place late on the evening of July 4, 1947. Conventional wisdom suggested the crash took place on July 2, but that, according to what William Moore wrote in *The Roswell Incident*, was based on the sighting by Dan Wilmot of an object over Roswell on July 2. There certainly was no reason to connect the debris reported by Mack Brazel with the UFO seen by Wilmot.

The Guards Go Out

When Kaufmann made his claim that the crash took place on July 4, it did make sense out of one aspect of the case. William Woody had told me that he and his father had seen the flying saucer fall toward the ground. When they went out to search for it along Highway 285, north of Roswell, and tried to turn off to the west, they found military police guarding the roads.

Under the conventional wisdom developed by Moore and others, this meant that Woody saw the object on a Wednesday and that he and his father waited until the following Tuesday, after Brazel had been into Roswell, before they went in search of the object. Under the information supplied by Kaufmann, the object fell on a Friday and the military cordon went up on Saturday. Woody and his father would have run into the guards the next day, rather than nearly a week later. Logically, it made more sense.

There is one other, similarly subtle corroboration. One of the MPs, interviewed by me nearly 50 years after the event, said that he hadn't been directly involved in the retrieval, either as a guard or participant. He did, however, hear his fellow MPs, returning to the barracks, talk of the flying saucer. He told me that he hadn't believed them until he read about it in the newspaper.

This means that there had been guards, cordons, and retrievals prior to

Brazel coming into town and prior to the publication of the information in the *Roswell Daily Record*. This corroborates the time line provided by Kaufmann and suggests that he was providing information based on his recollections rather than inventing a tale that was influenced by the publicity surrounding the Roswell case.

Kaufmann has offered some documentation to prove his involvement, though he has been tight-fisted in releasing any of it to researchers. In 1997, he showed me a letter, signed by Edwin Easley, the Roswell provost marshal in 1947, that, if verified, would end discussion about the UFO crash. Here was a document that made mention of the unusual nature of the material recovered, suggested that the bodies recovered did not appear to be human, and that the debris was unlike anything seen before or since. This document, if verified, was the smoking gun of ufology.

Kaufmann did not allow me to have a copy of it. I would have attempted to verify Easley's signature, verify the date of manufacture of the typewriter, and find other, similar documents. Although Kaufmann promised me a copy, I never received it. For researchers, the lack of copies renders the document useless. The existence of it is hearsay, and there is nothing to suggest that it is authentic.

I will note two things about that letter, however. I know precisely what it says, and I know that several others have seen it. This proves only that Kaufmann had such a letter and not that it was an authentic document signed by Easley.

Exaggeration of His Role?

And that sums up, nicely, the Kaufmann enigma. There are aspects of his story that seem to prove his veracity. There are subtle hints that he was telling the overall truth but that he might have stuck himself into the story in a role of greater importance than he had in 1947. At this point, there is no one to contradict him.

On the other hand, these little corroborations might be nothing more than coincidence. Kaufmann, having worked with General Scanlon, and unaware of his intelligence background, could have plugged him into the story because Scanlon was a real general and Kaufmann knew that he was long dead.

And, while Kaufmann might not have been overly familiar with the Roswell story when he was first identified in the early 1990s, by the middle of the decade he was well involved in it, having granted interviews to CBS and to a variety of foreign documentary makers. By 1997, he had become jaded, demanding money before he would sit down in front of a camera. Asking for compensation for an interview certainly does not invalidate the claims, but it sure raises suspicions in the minds of many.

With the Roswell case, some of the early witnesses, those that seemed to have solid tales, have fallen in recent years. Others have been challenged, but those challenges have often hinged on small, trivial discrepancies between a story told 10 or 15 years ago and one told today.

Kaufmann now skates with those with a semi-official status. He had been assigned to the Army, but as a civilian. He had been a master sergeant in the Army, but promoted to a GS-11 when he was assigned to Roswell as a civilian. The GS-11 is the civilian equivalent of a company grade officer. If he knew Scanlon, and the others brought in, if he had worked with them in the past, then it is easy to believe he would have been included because they knew who he was and knew that he could be trusted.

Kaufmann's tales remain almost totally uncorroborated. If he was who he claimed, then explanations for the Roswell crash, other than the extraterrestrial, are eliminated. If he is not, then one of the best witnesses, one who claimed to have specific inside knowledge, has been eliminated. I believe Kaufmann was who he claimed and that the Roswell crash was alien. At the moment, that makes the most sense.

Roswell and the Sci-Fi Channel

Kevin D. Randle
February 2003

J UST ABOUT THE TIME we begin to believe that we have found everything of value in the Roswell case, something new comes along and we have to reassess the information one more time. In recent weeks, there have been several new sources of information revealed, and each has provided us with clues about the truth surrounding what has become the most controversial of UFO cases. And there is something for everyone in all that new information, from corroboration suggesting that the crash was a real event and probably extraterrestrial, to proof that one of the important wit-

Recreated debris field used in the ShowTime original movie, *Roswell*.

nesses to the UFO crash was making up his story to center himself in the spotlight.

Probably the best source of new data is the Sci-Fi Channel's documentary, *The Roswell Crash: Startling New Evidence,* which began airing in late November 2002. The two-hour program covered some controversial old ground with new interviews and then broke away from that story in an attempt to bring some science to the UFO phenomenon. The documentary summarized what was best about the new information being developed and gave a balanced look into the Roswell case without tripping into the sensational. It was centered on the debris field which had been identified for me in 1989 by Bill Brazel, son of Mack Brazel, the man who found the debris in 1947. Later, in what would become an important bit of corroboration, Bud Payne would take me, along with several others, out to where he had seen the strange metallic debris in 1947. Payne said that he had been chased from the area by the military police. Payne's identification of the debris field corroborated the location provided by Bill Brazel.

Don Schmitt (left) and Bill Brazel after an interview conducted in 1989.

Brazel's Testimony

Bill Brazel sat down with Don Schmitt and me in early 1989 to give us his impressions of what he had seen and what his father had told him. He made it clear that his father had promised the government not to talk about it and, according to Bill, he was the kind of man who lived up to his word. Bill only heard a couple of things, one of which was that the debris looked as if it had fallen out of the sky, and there was so much of it that the older Brazel wondered who was going to clean up the mess. That had been his motivation for going into Roswell and for telling the sheriff what he had found.

Later, after his father returned to the ranch, Bill learned a little about what had happened. Bill said that in the months that followed, when riding that part of the ranch, he would find small bits of strange metallic debris. He showed some of it to his father, who said it looked like part of the contraption he had found.

In 1989, Bill Brazel described that material for Schmitt and me. If Brazel's

The debris field as identified by both Bill Brazel and
Bud Payne. The gouge ran for about 500 feet down the center.

description of the material is accurate, then terrestrial explanations fall away. He told Schmitt and me, "There were three items involved. Something on the order of balsa wood, and something on the order of heavy gauge monofilament fishing line and a little piece of...it wasn't really aluminum foil and it really wasn't lead foil but it was on that order." While the descriptions sound vaguely familiar, Brazel quickly moved them out of that area telling us that the "balsa wood" was so strong that he could not cut it with his knife. The fishing line was more like fiber optics. Brazel mentioned that he could shine a light in one end and it came out the other.

It was the foil that had the most otherworldly properties. According to Brazel, he could roll it into a ball and let go of it. It would return to its original shape. He suggested that when he folded it into a tiny square, it would unfold itself and there would be no sign of a wrinkle or a crease.

Brazel showed that debris to others, including neighbor Sallye Tadolini. In an affidavit she completed for the Fund for UFO Research, she said, "It felt like no fabric I have touched before or since...when I crumpled it in my hands, the feel was like that you notice when you crumple a leather glove. When it was released, it sprang back into its original shape, quickly flattening out with no wrinkles."

Brazel told us that sometime later, he was visited by four Air Force officers and enlisted men. He said that they weren't there to confiscate the debris, but they made it clear they weren't going to leave without it. He surrendered it to them, but not before telling them it was like nothing he had ever seen.

Site of the Debris Field

After hearing these descriptions, we were interested in learning exactly where the debris had been found. Brazel agreed to take us out to where his father had made the discovery. To get there, we needed to drive cross country, west from a windmill where the sheep were watered, down into a shallow valley, and then up on a ridge. From there we could look down into another shallow valley. Brazel told us that the debris had been found there and that he had seen a gouge in the dirt, maybe 500 feet long and ten feet at its widest. It wasn't very deep, but it was clear, even months after the events. Brazel said that it took a year or two to grass back over.

The J. Allen Hynek Center for UFO Studies organized an archaeological expedition to that site in late summer 1989. For ten days, under the direction of two professional archaeologists, a number of us, using standard site-survey techniques, dug test holes, used shaker boxes, mapped, and searched for some sign of the events described in 1947. Although samples were taken, nothing ever came from the tests. But this was all preliminary. CUFOS hoped to return, but the money for a complete survey was never available.

The Sci-Fi Channel, in 2002, supplied not only the cash but arranged for a new archaeological dig directed by Dr. William Doleman, a scientist at the University of New Mexico, to be conducted on that same debris field, also known as the "skip site." Using standard archaeological site-survey techniques and newer, ground-penetrating radars, they searched for evidence of the crash. The assumption was that no matter how thoroughly the military might have tried to clean the site, bits of metal, maybe microscopic samples, would have escaped them. Small, burrowing animals might have carried fragments into their holes. Scraps might have become trapped in the roots of the older plants and then held there against the forces of nature. In other words, some remnants might be left, and if they could be found, then evidence about the nature of the craft could be discovered.

Samples were gathered into 66 brown paper bags, all labeled, dated, and stored in a bank vault. In fact, according to the documentary, there were armed guards on the site, checking the identities of those who came and went in an attempt to prevent "salting." It was never clear if they feared ufologists bringing in debris to be found, or skeptics who might bring in bits of a balloon to prove their theories. There was even discussion on the Internet about these sorts of attempts, but no evidence was presented, or found, that anyone tried to salt the site.

Weather Balloon

The archaeologists did find the remains of a weather balloon. With grass and other plant life growing through it, the archaeologists believed the balloon had been there for a number of years. It was a bright yellowish object that clearly was not the remnants of a neoprene balloon of the 1940s. Those older balloons began to turn dark upon exposure to the sun and in a matter of weeks turned brittle. They would disintegrate quickly. Analysis of this balloon, supplied by experts in the weather service, suggested the balloon was no more than a decade old. Clearly it had nothing to do with the events of 1947.

The Sci-Fi Channel's documentary, rather than spending a great deal of time on the old stories, touched on them only briefly, assuming the audience would know the rough outline of the case. Consequently, there was little of 1st Lt. Walter Haut, who had talked about writing the press release concerning the crashed saucer recovery. Haut's story has always been that

Glenn Dennis, who told of an Army nurse's story about the crash and the alien bodies.

he knew nothing more and that he wasn't even sure if he had composed the press release, or if Col. William Blanchard, commander of the 509th Bomb Group, had dictated it to him. Haut has suggested, in recent years, that he knows more about the case, including hints about the bodies recovered, but none of that knowledge has yet entered the public arena. He has created a videotaped record of these memories, but that tape has yet to be released.

There was very little of a wan-looking Glenn Dennis repeating his rather tired tale of the missing nurse. Many UFO researchers have tried to find the missing nurse with no results. Dennis has told his story many times and has provided researchers with what he claims are drawings of the alien creatures. Unfortunately, Dennis did not see them himself but had to rely on drawings created by the nurse in 1947. Although he claimed to have kept them, those original drawings have long since disappeared. Dennis gave me, in 1990, the drawing he had made, with the help of Walter Henn, that represented, to the best of his memory, what the nurse had shown him in

1947.

Tom Carey and Don Schmitt, who assisted in the archaeological dig for the Sci-Fi Channel and who identified the debris field based on what Brazel had told Schmitt and me a decade earlier, also went in search of a fallen, wooden windmill. This is the site where the craft and bodies were supposed to have been found and is based, partially, on testimony supplied by former Air Force Brig. Gen. Arthur Exon and new testimony from Frank Kaufmann and indirectly from Dee Proctor, son of Loretta. They didn't find any wooden windmill, either standing or fallen, but did find what they thought might be the remains of such a structure.

Carey and Schmitt, in covering old ground, seem to have developed some new and interesting leads. They described, in the Winter 1999 issue of the *International UFO Reporter,* that they had made contact with the family of the late Meyers Wahnee, who had told family members that bodies had been found and that there were three separate crash sites. The bodies were flown first to Texas and then on to other locations. Carey and Schmitt suggested that what was of special interest was "his testimony to his wife and children about decomposing body parts found among the debris at the Foster ranch."

New Evidence

The newest and the latest evidence revealed on the documentary falls into four distinct segments. First there was Moe Cox, who claimed that he had been assigned to Briggs Air Force Base in Texas, and at some point in his career, saw a Project Blue Book file that contained information and photographs of the crash. Cox said that the photographs and documents proved the Roswell crash to be real. He said that it was part of the Project Blue Book files held at the base.

The problem here is that we know, based on our surveys of the Blue Book files, that nothing relating to Roswell, with the exception of a single paragraph in the middle of a single newspaper clipping, is hidden there.

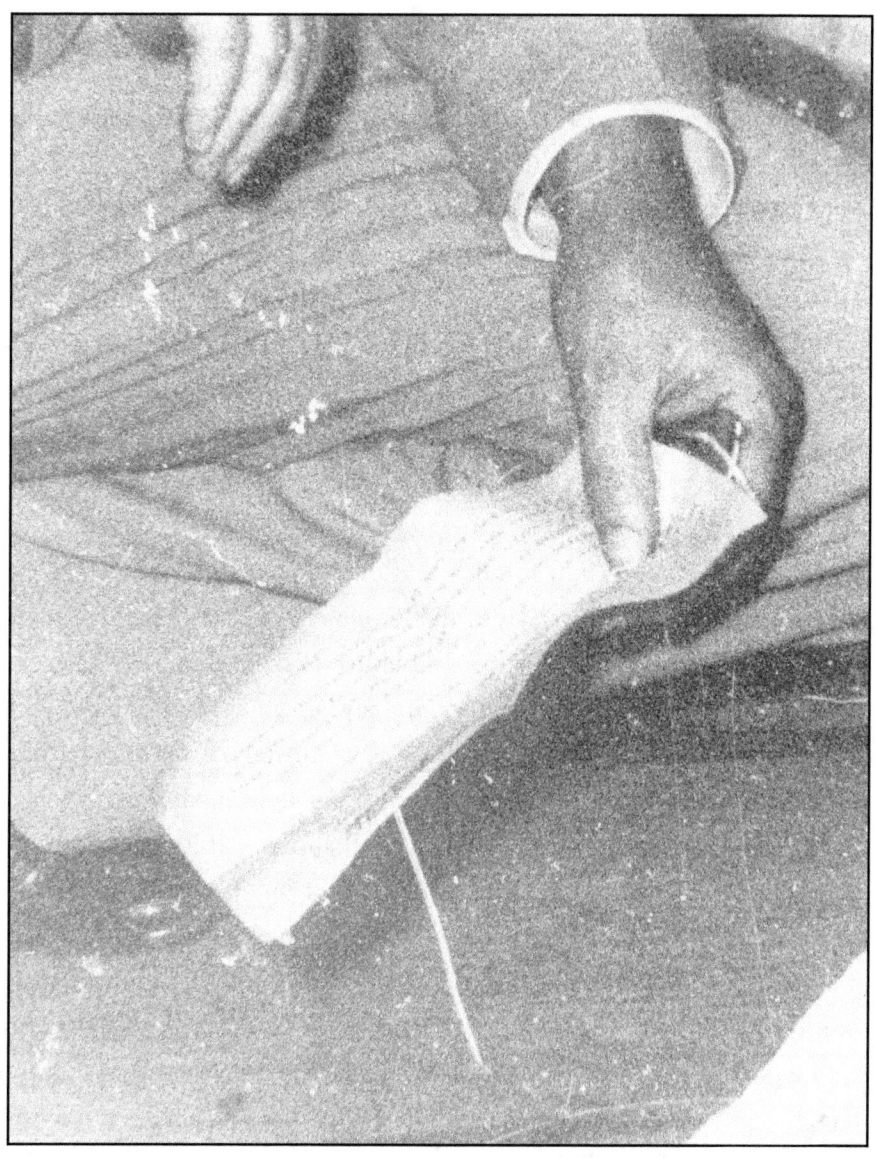

The memo held by Brig. Gen. Roger Ramey. The text
is visible, though the interpretation is open to question.

Cox might have mistakenly assumed that the files were part of the Blue Book system.

I have run into similar accounts in the past. One man told me of a file he had seen while stationed in the NORAD complex in Colorado that was labeled Army Air Force Early Automation that held data and photographs relating to a UFO crash. Given what we were learning about Roswell, he assumed, maybe incorrectly, that this file was related to the Roswell case. He didn't remember much about it, only that he had seen it.

The point is that neither of these stories has any supportive corroboration, and all fly in the face of military regulations. Neither Cox nor my source should have had access to the material they claim to have seen because, if true, the material would have been highly classified. Neither had the "need to know" to see it legally. But, as we dig deeper into Roswell, and into military secrecy, we learn that mistakes are sometimes made. It is possible that both men might have seen something they shouldn't have.

The second revelation, and one that ultimately might prove to be the most valuable, was the analysis of the Ramey memo conducted by David Rudiak. The Ramey memo is from a picture of Brig. Gen. Roger Ramey taken on July 8, 1947. In the picture, Ramey is seen holding a document, and blowups of the memo reveal vague and often distorted writing. Rudiak, as well as many other UFO researchers, have spent time trying to clarify and understand what is written on that paper. It is about the only document to surface from the Roswell case that isn't troubled by a lack of provenance. We know where the document originated because we have a picture of Ramey holding it, and we know that the photograph was taken in July 1947, because copies were printed in the newspapers of that time. Finally, we can pin down the date because records exist showing that the photograph was transmitted by wire from Fort Worth to a news service on the evening of July 8, 1947.

In the last several years, there have been attempts to read this memo, and that has led to various interpretations. There are some words that can be read without the aid of anything more significant than a magnifying glass. The message clearly refers to Fort Worth, Texas, and in another point, to weather balloons, though weather is misspelled.

Rudiak's Reading

Rudiak, using a variety of equipment and techniques, believes that he has now read the majority of the memo. If he has, and if he is correct in his assumptions, then we have a smoking gun. Rudiak's interpretation of the memo leads to the conclusion that something extraordinary crashed outside of Roswell.

According to Rudiak, one of the lines of the memo says, "Victims of the wreck." There is little room for interpretation of that sentence. And, because other aspects refer to weather balloons, Fort Worth, Texas, and even a disk, in quotation marks, and finally a mention of Roswell, Rudiak believes that the memo refers to the crash and that the note about victims means the alien crew.

But Rudiak is not the only researcher studying the Ramey memo or the only one to obtain interesting results. Don Burleson has been studying the Ramey memo for years and has used a wide variety of computer equipment and the latest in software. Burleson said, "He [Rudiak] agrees with the rest of us on such basic points as 'disk,' 'victims of the wreck,' etc. His reading of 'Ramey' as the signature line is demonstrably incorrect, as that is clearly a six-character group...But as I said, we all agree on some vital points."

What this suggests is that others, working from the same basic raw material, have discovered the same phrases in the Ramey memo. The unfortunate fact in this is that each of those working to understand the memo have been exposed to the same discussions, so that the discoveries are not completely independent. It can be argued that some contamination has taken place.

The director and one of the writers on the Sci-Fi Channel documentary, Melissa Jo Peltier, commented on the work done by Rudiak. She said, "I'm not a skeptic by any means—I'm completely open minded—but I am at a state, after a year on *Sightings* [a television exploration of the paranormal and UFOs], that no matter how much I want to believe, I really have to say, 'Show me.' And Rudiak's work impressed me on some levels."

The third revelation was that the archaeologists found the remnants of some kind of gouge on the debris field. An excavation by a backhoe exposed some kind of a trench that had been dug out and then filled back in. It is in the place identified by Bill Brazel to me years ago. This could be physical evidence of the craft touching, skipping, across the ground there.

Dr. Doleman, the lead archaeologist, was excited with what they found, but he also told reporters for an Albuquerque newspaper that the gouge could have been the remains of something more natural. But the fact remains, it was found where we had always believed the gouge would be.

Karl Pflock, however, reports that an aerial survey of the area conducted in 1946 suggests that the gouge found by Doleman and his crew might have been there earlier than the events of July 1947. Pflock, who wrote the skeptical *Roswell: Inconvenient Facts and the Will to Believe,* also said that Doleman told friends, and reporter John Fleck of the *Albuquerque Journal,* that the furrow could have been just about anything. In other words, evidence exists that might take the significance out of this one discovery. Research needs to be completed before there are conclusions.

Finally, proving that there was something for everyone in the documentary and in the research surrounding Roswell, the tales told by Frank Kaufmann were revealed publicly as a hoax. Although the Sci-Fi Channel didn't provide the documentation, it does exist and was published by the Center for UFO Studies on their website four days after the documentary first aired. There had been deep suspicions voiced by some about the quality of the information supplied by Kaufmann, while his evidence was accepted by others. This was the first public revelation by supporters that Kaufmann could no longer be considered reliable.

Rudiak, arguing that some of what Kaufmann said might be true, reported on *UFO Updates* that even when Kaufmann "…was dying, frail, and deathly ill, he was still going to take Carey and Schmitt out to the 'true' main craft crash site. According to Carey, they were all in the Land Rover ready to go when an unseasonable snowstorm prevented the trip at the last moment."

But what this would mean was that Kaufmann was about to show them the fourth crash site. First was one that he described, the second he had taken Schmitt to, the third he had taken Schmitt and me to, and now the fourth site that was somewhat closer to the debris field.

It should be noted that the third site Kaufmann identified for us was well documented, at least by him. He pointed to mountain peaks in the distance, and how two of them stuck up, providing, according to Kaufmann, a landmark for those looking for the site. He had drawings of mountains, seen on one of the documents he gave me, that showed, roughly, where the site was.

We Don't Know It All

What all this means is that there are still things to be learned. Some of it is not a happy circumstance for researchers. The recent revelations about Frank Kaufmann are, naturally, a setback for those who accept the extraterrestrial nature of the Roswell case. Some of the new revelations are dubious in their importance, simply because they come from second— and third-— hand sources. Those sorts of stories are open to interpretation and misunderstanding by those hearing them.

Of significance is the study of the Ramey memo. Here is where the smoking gun can be found, if proper scientific protocols are observed and the results can be universally duplicated. For those asking where is the documentation, it might be that there is now an answer. It might be that General Ramey is holding it.

(For more information on the Ramey Memo and the Roswell case, see *The Roswell Encyclopedia* by Kevin D. Randle and *A Message in a Bottle: Confounds in Deciphering the Ramey Memo from the Roswell Case* by James Houran and Kevin D. Randle.)

Archaeological Site Survey of the Debris Field

Kevin D. Randle
February 2003

WILLIAM DOLEMAN, PH.D., of the University of New Mexico, was contracted by the Sci-Fi Channel to conduct an archaeological site survey of what is known as the debris field. This is an area on what was, in 1947, a huge ranch owned by the Foster family and on which Mack Brazel worked as the foreman. I had the chance to ask Dr. Doleman some questions about his research. He provided some detailed and interesting answers.

According to what he said, the research was conducted over more than two weeks in a very isolated area of central New Mexico. He said, "We spent eight days setting up our grid system and mapping the site (six before the volunteers arrived and two after), and four days supervising the volunteers. I also spent two days evaluating the backhoe trenches and doing detailed soil-stratigraphy studies."

The documentary suggested that one of the most significant finds was a trench or furrow that might have been caused as something skipped across the ground. About these areas, Dr. Doleman said, "I found two possible 'furrow' features. One was in the side of a backhoe trench in the area where we worked. The trench was one of three excavated across the 'initial impact point' as determined by Don Schmitt, who based his determination on his having been taken to it by eyewitnesses."

These would be both Bill Brazel and Bud Payne. Tommy Tyree, who worked with Brazel in 1947, added some insight as to the location and the size of the debris field.

"This feature mostly disappeared when I scraped the trench profile, but the backhoe excavator claims he 'felt it' through the controls of his machine, and also detected it visually and by probing it when he got out of his backhoe to inspect it. Because he is an archeological backhoe expert with 20 years' experience with whom I've worked many times before (it's why I recommended him), I tend to believe him. A follow-up excavation would be required to determine for good the feature's existence and origin.

"The other, 'alternative furrow,' was found half a mile to the east-southeast of the test excavation area and is ironically almost directly online (a) with the furrow alignment Don showed me, and (b) with the line that connects the Schmitt-Carey skip site where we worked and their final crash site some 17 miles away. This feature looks very 'furrow-like' and shows up on aerial photography from both 1954 and 1946.

"The final irony is that there was a high-altitude payload balloon some 100 meters to the south of this feature. This item may or may not be a weather balloon, as there are a variety of other government and university high-altitude experiments that use such balloons. Folks at the Albuquerque National Weather Service 'guessed' that the balloon couldn't be more than ten years old, but could not say for certain. As the payloads these balloons carry are generally less than a pound, the balloon's payload could not have created the 'alternative furrow.' Just a tremendously ironic coincidence, I guess."

I asked about the most significant thing they found while they were out there. Dr. Doleman said, "With the exception of the as-yet-unanalyzed soil samples and HMOUs (Historic Materials of Uncertain Origin, our term for any unidentified, non-Native American and non-natural things that popped up in the sifting screens), it was the backhoe trench feature we discussed."

As noted, they collected samples into 66 bags, sealed them, and stored them in a bank vault. Naturally, I was curious about the status of that material and if any of it had been analyzed. I knew up front that Dr. Doleman might not be able to tell me everything that had been found, but hoped to get an update about what was in those bags. I asked, "Has any of the material in the bags been analyzed and is there a date when we can expect to hear something?"

Dr. Doleman said, "Larry Landsman at Sci-Fi tells me that they do want to follow up with analysis of the currently locked-up soil samples and HMOUs. But they have yet to pursue it."

Finally, Dr. Doleman, responding to some of the other investigations being pursued, and some of the questions raised about the archaeological dig, said, "I can guarantee that there was no bias on our part, and I will gladly defend my and my office's scientific credentials to anybody who might question them."

Which seems to tell us that Dr. Doleman entered into this with no bias or agenda of his own. His research was conducted using the proper scientific protocols and research techniques. It demonstrates that science can be brought to bear on many aspects of the Roswell question. Until the results of the analysis have been completed and Dr. Doleman files his final report, all we know for certain are that some interesting things turned up during the work.

Roswell Was Real
But are the briefings and the artifacts?

Rosemary Ellen Guiley
UFO Special, 2005

"Roswell was a real incident—bodies and materials were recovered, and it was investigated by MJ-12."

So asserted astronaut Edgar Mitchell at the July 2004 UFO Festival in Roswell, New Mexico. Roswell has been at the center of continuing controversy in ufology since July 2, 1947, when an alien craft allegedly crashed nearby. Was it really a UFO, or was it something else—maybe even a weather balloon, as the government quickly claimed? Mitchell sided with the belief of most ufologists that an alien vehicle did crash, and both live and dead extraterrestrials and craft artifacts were recovered by the military.

The Cover-up Is Real

Mitchell, who grew up in Roswell and nearby Artesia, became the sixth American astronaut to walk on the moon in 1971. He told his audience at the Roswell Civic Center that he has never had a firsthand UFO experience. He said he has become convinced of the reality of ETs from briefings and testimonials he has received from individuals in government, military, and intelligence circles. He described some of his sources as "old timers" who had longstanding knowledge about ET events, plus a source of "recent vintage in a very high position in the military." This source thought he should have oversight on UFO and alien matters and undertook an investigation. Mitchell said the source found out things were going on right under his nose, but he was told that he could have no access to them.

"He and another source confirmed that some of these events are very real—there is equipment, there are aliens, there have been bodies in our grasp, in our laboratories." Mitchell said he was convinced of reverse engineering of alien craft, and that much of what is reported in the ufology literature of sightings and contacts is home-grown.

Mitchell added that not every event reported is true, and some of the data associated with various events may not be true. He said he could not give more details without compromising his sources.

Mitchell said he was disturbed at the history of government cover-up. There may have been a rationale for it 50 years ago, but not now. "It's hard to know when we're going to be able to crack this. Sooner or later, it's going to break open." Mitchell does not know how to break open the cover-up. He has tried to do so, traveling to Washington, D.C., to brief members of Congress and White House staff. "They listen and then they go away and do nothing."

Mitchell said that John F. Kennedy was the last president to have significant knowledge of the truth about ETs. "He probably had a pretty good handle on what's going on. Those since then don't, and those who have asked have been rebuffed."

Resistance from the mainstream media has been a problem ever since the Roswell incident. "We basically have the press against us."

Spending tax money year after year on secret programs without public oversight is criminal, Mitchell said. He fears the country is heading toward more dictatorial control and loss of freedom. "We have to see what we can do as citizens to keep pressing the case." He advocated that people work on their own consciousness, and understand how to use the power of intentionality. "When we know how to get ourselves together and create intentionality, we can move the world."

Edgar Mitchell and Phyllis Galde at 2004 Roswell UFO Festival.
photo by Paul Davids

Mitchell had a mystical experience during the return of the Apollo 14 mission, in which he realized that his atoms, as well as the atoms of his fellow crew mates and other humans, are fused with the ancient atoms of the stars. In 1972, he founded the Institute of Noetic Sciences, based in Sausalito, California, to pursue scientific research of mystical and spiritual experiences, and the mind-body connection.

Smoke and Mirrors

The mixture of fact and disinformation about ETs and UFOs referred to by Edgar Mitchell has plagued modern ufology since its post-World War II beginnings. Information and documents about MJ-12 (a.k.a. Majestic-12) came to light in the 1980s, via William Moore (co-author of *The Roswell Inci-*

dent, 1980, with Charles Berlitz), Moore's associate Jamie Shandera, and two military sources: Sgt. Richard C. Doty of the Air Force Office of Special Investigations at Kirtland Air Force Base near Albuquerque, and former U.S. Air Force captain Robert Collins. In 1984 Shandera received anonymously a roll of 35-millimeter film of photographs of an alleged briefing paper from Adm. Roscoe H. Hillenkoetter to President-Elect Dwight D. Eisenhower, dated November 18, 1952. According to the paper, Operation Majestic-12 was secretly established by President Harry S Truman in 1947 to investigate the Roswell crash and oversee ET issues. Its 12 members included top scientists, intelligence personnel, and military officers. The paper established the term "Extraterrestrial Biological Entities," or "EBEs" as the designated term for aliens. A copy of the briefing paper also was leaked to British ufologist Timothy Good.

Its authenticity debated, the paper nonetheless became a centerpoint in the UFO cover-up controversy. In 1989 Moore spoke at the annual MUFON conference and admitted to having participated in a disinformation counterintelligence operation. He said he thought that some of the information he had passed along to ufologists was true.

More documents related to MJ-12, its members, and its activities have been publicly disclosed and examined; some have been determined to be false. (For more information on the complexities of MJ-12, see the forensics work of Robert Wood and Ryan Wood, sponsors of the UFO Crash Retrieval conferences in Las Vegas, at *www.majesticdocuments.com*.)

ET Briefings

About three months after the 2004 Roswell festival, a former high-ranking employee of the Central Intelligence Agency admitted privately to receiving four briefings about aliens over a period of years, FATE learned.

The ex-employee said the briefings took place around 1984 in a Pentagon SCIF (Sensitive Compartmented Information Facility, a room electromagnetically sealed and used for top secret briefings), in 1987 at a western U.S. military base, in 1999 at a private location in Florida, and in September 2004 at an undisclosed location in Washington, D.C. The briefings were given by an unspecified GS-14 employee, a colonel and a captain in the U.S. Air Force, and a past assistant to the Secretary of Defense. The ex-CIA employee said that the briefings included information on reverse engineering.

An analyst who has worked for the CIA and who has open interests in such subjects as ufology, crop circles, free energy, and passive coherent radar, has opined privately that these briefings may be part of a smoke screen of deception, or a decoy. According to another source, this analyst has said that he is aware of dozens of such alleged briefings, but that he has been unable to find connections between the known briefers. Typically there would be a single, low-echelon staff person at a given facility involved, but the supervisor would claim to be unaware of the briefing.

The ex-CIA employee who was briefed said he had no problem with this as a broad interpretation, but that there was a core story that remained consistent.

The question remains: what is the true core story?

Testing the Artifacts

Meanwhile, a controversy heated up over the test results of an alleged crash artifact. While giving a presentation at the Roswell UFO Museum and Research Center for the July festival, veteran ufologist Stanton T. Friedman was given a small piece of thin metal retrieved in June 2004 from the Plains of San Agustin northwest of Roswell, where a second UFO crash was believed to have happened at about the same time as the Roswell-Corona crash in July 1947.

The artifact was presented by Chuck Wade, who surprised Friedman and his fellow panelists Don Schmitt and Tom Carey by coming forward from the audience. Wade is a retired civil engineer living in Gallup, New Mexico, who has been investigating the crash incidents.

Friedman had the metal analyzed at a California forensics laboratory with whom he has worked in the past. The assessment on the sample was that it was a dirty piece of ordinary aluminum. A concentration of silicon was present on the uncleaned surface but not on the cleaned surface. The silicon apparently was in the dirt embedded on the metal's surface.

Wade later took issue with the results during a presentation he gave at the second annual UFO Crash Retrieval Conference in Las Vegas in November 2004. He had six other metal artifacts retrieved from the same dig site sent to New Mexico Institute of Mining and Technology in Socorro for testing. The results told a different story: an apparently anomalous composition of aluminum and silicon that could not be attributed to surface dirt.

Wade grew up in Corona, and his father knew Mac Brazel, the rancher who found the original crash debris. Wade himself knew Brazel's sons. Wade was guided to search in the Plains of San Agustin by Art Campbell, an Oregon researcher who had presented on his artifact finds in the plains at the first UFO Crash Retrieval Conference in Las Vegas in 2003 and the UFO symposium in Aztec, New Mexico in March 2004.

Wade's June 2004 dig involved nine people, including Campbell. The group found several pieces of apparent aluminum alloy ranging from 17 microns to 1,500 microns in thickness.

The six pieces sent for analysis ranged from 17 to 65 microns in thickness. Wade said their content was tested according to cross sections. One piece 30 microns in thickness was analyzed at 91 percent aluminum, 6 percent iron, and 3 percent silicon. Household aluminum foil is 17 microns thick and typically is 98.5 percent aluminum and 1.5 percent other ingredients, he said. "The silicon [in the artifact] did not come from the soil—I want to stress that," he said.

Wade believes the piece given to Friedman should be re-analyzed.

The Other Paradigm

E. A. Guest
April 2005

FOR TOO MANY YEARS, people have wondered about the truth in the so-called "Roswell Incident," which, according to conventional wisdom, is the classic event surrounding the extraterrestrial hypothesis as answer to the UFO question. For many of those years, I have wondered myself, though the answer was there all along, waiting to be uncovered.

My personal odyssey with the Roswell Incident began before I ever heard the term, and it came in the wake of discussion on another interesting chapter in UFO history. I lived in Mineral Wells, West Virginia, during the years of strange activity there, including the notorious Mothman visitations. But we returned to California in the late 1960s. I was very young and do not consciously recall that far back in my life.

When we returned to West Virginia in 1973, our neighbors were old family friends, Hilda and Peanuts Sartor. They had known my grandparents. It was Hilda who first mentioned the name of Indrid Cold, the UFO occupant allegedly associated with the Mothman sightings.

Indrid Cold

The Sartors knew something of the Indrid Cold saga. Their daughter-in-law Darla was mentioned often in John Keel's *The Mothman Prophecies*. Naturally, talk of Cold opened the table to UFOs and what they might be, where they might come from. Like everyone else, I was quite charmed by the idea that they came from outer space. It seemed the most logical source. Because my father had been in the Air Force, and my family had spent so much time enjoying science fiction movies, it was a popular subject around our house.

Sometime in 1974, I first heard about the crash of a craft in the desert of New Mexico. My father had always displayed an open mind where UFOs were concerned. He told me that something had crashed in the desert of New Mexico several years before. He encouraged my sisters and me to consider the possibility that there were other people and other worlds. The discussion would often meander into other avenues, and the crash allusion would fade or end. But it always returned.

I would learn of other things that would always return in later years.

Fascinated by UFOs

By 1977, I was avidly fascinated with the subject of UFOs, and enamored with the extraterrestrial hypothesis. That year, a movie hit the theaters that deeply affected my life: *Close Encounters of the Third Kind*. From that point on, my father's story became more detailed.

That was the first year he described the aliens to me: they looked like us, but with little or no body hair. He insisted that the ETs in Spielberg's film were not what the bodies looked like at all. I asked if he had seen them and that was the first time I heard the story I will relate later in this article, because it included more detail with the tellings over the years. I will also share with you the reason for that.

The Myth Contradicted

The story I would hear from my father was consistent, and it contradicted much of what the UFO industry has espoused for over 20 years. Often, certain details would come out in his telling, and years later, some of these details would arise from the UFO community as "latest revelations"—but always filtered through the ET hypothesis. I would do my own research into certain aspects and find new angles from which to question my father. The information I pulled out of him either corroborated what little research does not follow the ET cult mantra, or, at the very least contradicted UFO legend. As time passed and I got better at subtle interrogation techniques, more details came out of our talks. These details have yet to ape any current trends in the UFO lore, and often precede some trends.

My father is scared to death that they are going to kill him if he tells too much. I have closely watched his personal emotional reaction to what he is relating to me. It can't be faked. Not by him.

The following is a brief version of what I have been told about the Roswell Incident and the bigger story involved in it.

In the late 1950s, my father served in the U.S. Air Force. He was assigned to a physiological training unit. His work involved training pilots in altitude chambers. He was also involved in the U.S. space program. His unit performed altitude chamber tests on the Mercury program pressure suits (those silver suits you see in *The Right Stuff*). He was stationed at George Air Force Base much of this time, but was doing flight medicine training at Gunter AFB in Montgomery, Alabama, at the time the events happened.

Trip to Wright-Patterson

My father's unit was selected for a special project that had them on a plane headed for a base in Texas. There were only a few of them on this plane; he's never told me the exact number. After taking off from Gunter, the plane banked north somewhere over Mississippi. An Air Force intelligence officer whom he identified as Major Knight came out into the cabin and told them they were actually flying to Wright-Patterson Field (AFB) in Ohio. Their public personnel records, they were told, would forever reflect a flight to Texas.

At Wright-Patterson, my father and his colleagues were briefed on what crashed in New Mexico in 1947. It did not actually crash in the popular Roswell location, and it was not an extraterrestrial spacecraft. They were shown debris, including the legendary aluminum-foil-like material that could be balled up and retained its shape. He says this material could not even be marked with extreme heat.

They were shown the bodies retrieved from the crash. Those bodies were "human," without hair. They did not have oversized heads. They did not have big black eyes. They were not little three-foot- tall extraterrestrials. He laughs every time the images of the "Greys" are connected with this incident. The ET depicted in recent Roswell material elicits head-shaking amusement from him. He insists that the occupants on the craft were human. He also insists that the cover-up of the event is senseless, as these people do not mean us harm in any way.

Following the time at Wright-Patterson, my father and the other men selected for this special assignment found themselves in Arizona—or, rather, under Arizona—in the vicinity of Winslow.

The special assignment team was attached to a project led by a civilian scientist named Wilson. This man delegated a security task to my father's group in connection with a search-and-rescue operation. Another craft had gone down in the Southwest and an occupant survived. This occupant, human in appearance, was lost, and his people wanted him back. They had contacted our authorities for assistance. They made it clear they were not interested in our world and merely wanted help in retrieving their man.

My father, who had been trained to fly helicopters in unusual places including underground caverns and tunnels, was assigned to an effort headed by Wilson to find and retrieve the lost crewman of the crashed craft.

Notice I did not say "spacecraft." It was not a spacecraft that brought the lost crewman to our world. Nor was it a spacecraft that crashed in the famous Roswell Incident.

An Inside Job

According to my father, these vehicles came from inside the planet. The civilization to which the crewman belonged exists in a vast, underground system of caverns and tunnels beneath the Southwest and is human. They went underground thousands of years ago.

Along with this civilization, there is a group of people who are blind, but have developed their other senses. My father's patrol encountered some of these people. One member of his team was killed by one of these blind ones, with a device the blind man held in his hand and pointed at the victim. The device works in conjunction with the mind. When my father told me this part of the story the first time, he broke down in tears. One moment the team member standing beside him was alive, and the next moment the man just dropped like a sack of potatoes, dead before he hit the ground.

This experience is what led my father to leave the Air Force when his service commitment was up. But it still haunts him.

I was told by another source that the method used to prevent witnesses such as my father from talking about their experiences was hypnosis keyed to the cycles of the Moon. As time goes on, its effect wears off. When the memory returns, the fear of being killed works to keep them from talking too much.

Intra-Terrestrials

This is the truth about the Roswell Incident according to my father. A civilization thrives underground, hidden from the surface world. The people there want nothing to do with our world, and are quite prepared to defend their position. These people are not extraterrestrials. Quite the contrary, they are among the oldest peoples on this planet. They, too, once lived on the surface until a cataclysmic event drove them underground. Occasionally, they come and go, emerging in their vehicles, and occasionally they crash. They are human in appearance, so much so that they can move among us with ease with just a little effort. If you got a close look, you'd notice something odd, but not if the person just passed you on the street. They mean us no harm, but are not interested in interaction either.

My father finds it aggravating that the UFO issue is used as a scare tactic on the public, and that the events he witnessed are being kept secret after so many decades, under a pretense of national security. For many centuries, expanding civilizations would find people living on lands believed not to exist. These newly discovered cultures were reported back home, and our understanding of the world was enriched. But now we live in an era where those with knowledge are handling it as a jealously guarded secret.

There will be those who will laugh, those who will spew venom, and those who will superstitiously cling to the mantra of the True Believer. The sellers of ET paraphernalia and literature will lead the charge against what I write here, for obvious reasons of profit. I don't really care if the cottage industry that has grown up in the New Age era of UFO research goes down in flames. It's stale. It hasn't produced anything convincing or truly revelatory in years. The ET hypothesis has kept UFO research stagnant for a long time.

I believe that the ET hypothesis has been used by the "aliens" themselves, since it is most readily embraced by people who have had encounters with them.

My advice to ufologists: Get over Roswell. Look at it in a different way. Expand your vistas of research. Recognize that there is as much historical material supporting the hidden race hypothesis as there is supporting the ET theory. This historical material, in many ways, is better evidence than that presented in support of the beloved alien mythos. Just imagine what truths we could uncover if this new theory was explored.

Plenty of Room

Take a look at a satellite image of the Earth at night, anywhere on the globe. Note where the concentrations of light are located. Then note the vast areas of darkness on this planet, representing areas that have few people, or none. Consider how easy it might be for a hidden race to move about on this planet without being noticed.

Take a drive across the Southwest, particularly Interstate 10, at night.

You might come away with a different point of view about who occupies this planet.

Roswell Explained—Again

Kevin D. Randle
September 2005

THE ROSWELL UFO CRASH CASE has been solved—yet again. Nick Redfern, writing in his new book, *Body Snatchers in the Desert*, has proposed a somewhat new but not extraterrestrial explanation. He suggests that what fell in Roswell was an American high-altitude experiment that contained the deformed and mutated bodies of Japanese captured at the close of World War II. The object that carried them was a huge balloon modeled after the balloon bombs launched during the war and a wooden flying-wing-type craft designed by the German Horten brothers that was taken from the Nazis.

Redfern suggests that those who found the wreckage, the officers at the

Gerald Anderson, who claimed that he had seen the crashed UFO on the Plains of San Agustin when he was five, identified this as the location. His story was uncorroborated and later dismissed.

Roswell Army Air Field, did not immediately identify the craft because of the weird construction, the aluminized rubber that made up the balloon, and other elements that seemed to defy easy explanation. The craft had carried five pilots (or possibly four), all killed in the crash. As the strange contraption broke up, a segment about nine meters long had fallen away. One of the pilots was sucked out the craft as it came apart, and this is what Mack Brazel found on the ranch he managed near Corona, New Mexico.

This experiment, designed to expose the captured Japanese to high altitudes to find out what would happen to the human body, could not be revealed to the general public. At the time, July 1947, the United States was trying Nazis in Nuremberg for crimes against humanity. Some of those crimes included experimentation on human subjects without their consent. Now, according to Redfern's theory, the United States had done the same thing. It would be the height of hypocrisy if the United States were engaged in the same sort of human experimentation.

Redfern's hypothesis does explain, to some extent, the various aspects

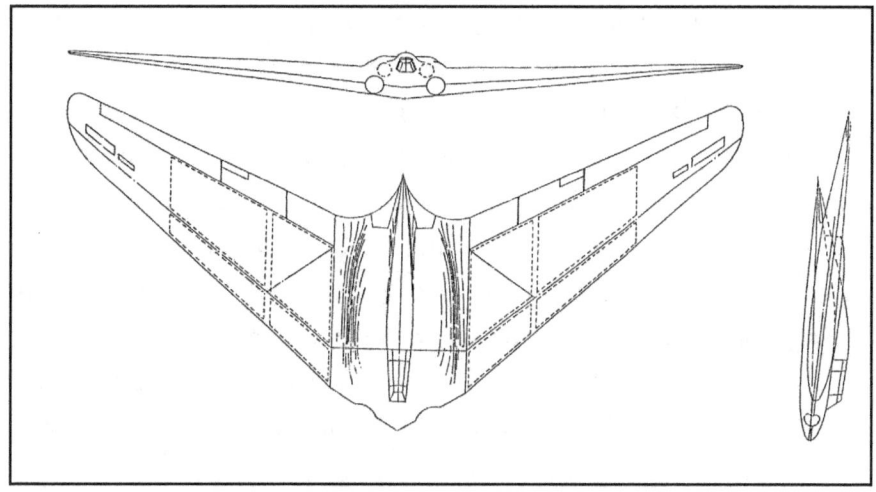

One of the many Horten Brothers flying wings. There is no evidence that any of them were brought to the United States.

of the Roswell case. It has a nice theory for the two crash locations; it explains why the government, in this case the military, would work so hard to hide the facts even today; and it explains the small bodies claimed to have been seen by so many of the witnesses in the Roswell case.

Flying Wings

However, I'm not sure why the Horten Brothers flying wing designs have been dredged up again. During the 1930s and 1940s, these two German brothers worked on what were thought of as tailless aircraft. They had 10 or 12 different designs, some of which crashed after only a few flying hours and others that were thought to have been scheduled for mass production but never were.

The Nazis needed a long-range bomber that could reach the United States, and one or two of the Horten brothers' designs were supposed to have had the range. At the close of World War II, the Horten brothers' aircraft plants were overrun by the Soviets. Nearly everything was carted back to the Soviet Union, and there was speculation that the Soviets would build as many as 1,800 Horten flying wings as a bomber force to counter the United States' buildup of long-range strategic bombers.

In the United States there was a similar flying wing project created by Jack Northrop prior to World War II. The plan also called for the development of a long-range bomber, but other priorities and technical problems kept it from completion. After the war, a four-engine version was created that flew a number of times. In June and July 1947, these aircraft were grounded with gearbox problems, effectively removing them as one explanation for the flying saucer reports made at the time.

Although the Northrop flying wing was suggested as a possible source of the Roswell debris, there was never any evidence that it was. Some believed the flying wing might have been responsible for the sighting of nine strange objects on June 24, 1947, by Kenneth Arnold that launched the modern UFO era. But again, the craft were grounded at the time and there were fewer than nine of them in the arsenal.

One of the Horten brothers' designs known as the Parabola certainly looks like the object Arnold sketched in the years after his sighting. The problem is that the first drawings Arnold made, in the days after the sighting, look little like the Parabola. And, again, there is no evidence that any of the Horten designs were brought to the United States, or that anything designed by the Hortens was built here.

Japanese Balloons

That takes us back to the Japanese, and what were called the balloon bombs. Starting in 1944 and continuing into 1945, the Japanese launched about 9,000 of these devices. The Japanese had discovered the jet stream and realized that a balloon launched in Japan would reach the Western Hemisphere, most probably the United States, in two or three days. If they put bombs on the balloons, along with some instruments, they could conceivably attack the United States.

The trick actually worked. Balloons launched in Japan rose during the day and fell during the night. Sandbags were attached and programmed

The two-engine version of the Northrop Flying Wing. By June 1947, all versions had either crashed or were no longer flying.

to drop if the balloon dipped too low. This way it maintained its altitude. After cycling two or three times, the bombs would fall. The Japanese knew that the odds were that the bombs would not hit a city, but did make plans to drop incendiary devices in the Pacific Northwest, hoping to start forest fires.

Records indicate that about 250 balloon bombs reached the Western Hemisphere, falling as far north as Canada, as far south as Mexico City, and as far east as Michigan. Any damage done was of little consequence.

The U.S. Office of Censorship, a wartime creation, working along with the FBI, suppressed the story during the war. They believed that Japanese spies, seeing the public information, would report home, telling of the success. That would increase the number of balloons launched.

The censorship worked well, but was changed when six people in Oregon—a woman and five children on a picnic—were killed when a bomb detonated. They had found one of the balloons lying in the forest and pulled on it, causing one of the bombs to explode. At that point a "whispering" campaign began to alert the population about the bombs.

While the ingenuity of the project can't be questioned, it was still a balloon. The technology to create the balloons wasn't special, and in fact, wasn't all that advanced. There is no reason to suspect that Japanese balloon technology was married with Horten flying wing technology to create some sort of hybrid.

Gerald Brown's Theories

This wasn't the first time that such a theory had been suggested, at least in general terms. Back in the early 1990s, as I began my research into the Roswell crash, I interviewed a man who worked with NASA at the White Sands Missile Range. Gerald Brown suggested that experiments using the A-9, a two-stage modified V-2 rocket, might have been responsible for the debris found by Mack Brazel. He believed that Duraluminum might explain the lightweight, thin metal that had been described by Roswell Army Air Field intelligence officer Maj. Jesse Marcel, Sr.

In fact, Brown had an explanation for everything found on the ranch with the exception of the bodies. He did speculate, suggesting that some kind of flying wing had crashed while carrying five chimpanzees dressed in silver flying suits. Since the experiment related to the space race, and since launch operations at White Sands had been closed down because of an accident in May 1947, those involved hid their mistake. They feared for their jobs. All this was laid out in my book, *UFO Crash at Roswell,* on pages 168 to 170.

The problem here was, again, no flying wing was missing from the inventories, there was no record of such a launch at White Sands (though the records did exist for the period), and there were no reports that animals had been killed in the tests. A year later, as experiments were designed and made to test the rigors of launch physics and the dangers of upper atmosphere flight, animals were launched. Those records also exist.

Rumors and stories of experiments pre-existed the revelations of Redfern. In fact, I have told many people that if I could find evidence of an illegal experiment that resulted in the deaths of human subjects, it would be a much bigger story, at least in terms of what the journalistic community would be willing to believe. Too many reject the idea of an alien spacecraft crash out of hand. But discover, and prove, some sort of underhanded experiment by the government, and nearly everyone would jump on board.

The problem for me was the lack of anything substantial. The records that I had examined at White Sands, in Alamogordo, at the National Archives, at the Southwest History Museum in Roswell, and at the universities and government offices in Albuquerque and Santa Fe revealed nothing to lead in that direction.

Maj. Jesse Marcel, Sr., walked the debris field and handled the wreckage. His descriptions of the debris seem to rule out terrestrial explanations.

Then there was the debris described by the witnesses, including Jesse Marcel, Sr.; Bill Brazel, son of Mack; Loretta Proctor; and Sallye Tadolini, whose mother, Marian Strickland, had been a neighbor of the Brazels in the summer of 1947. If we stick to these descriptions, then a terrestrially manufactured machine, even an experimental craft, seems less likely.

Exotic Debris

In an interview conducted in February 1989, Bill Brazel told me about the exotic debris he had found on the ranch: "The only reason I noticed the foil was that I picked this stuff up and put it in my chaps pocket. I had it in there, two, three days and when I took it out and put it in the box I happened to notice that it started unfolding and flattened out.... I would crease it and lay it down and watch it."

Brazel also described a small piece of debris as light as balsa wood but incredibly strong. He tried to whittle on it, but couldn't even get a sliver, suggesting something much tougher than anything used in a balloon. He mentioned something like fiber optics: "Now there's this plastic they put a light down one end and it transfers the light down that thing and come out the end." None of the items he described (other than fiber optics) appears in today's world.

Brazel's father Mack told him, "That looks like some of the contraption I found." That statement connected the strange debris to the descriptions of the others, such as Jesse Marcel.

Sallye Strickland Tadolini was a young girl in 1947. Bill Brazel, about a decade older, showed up at the Strickland ranch house a few days after the crash. He had the strange foil with him and let the others look at and play with it.

Tadolini, in an affidavit for the Fund for UFO Research, described it this way: "What Bill showed us was a piece of what I still think of as fabric. It was something like aluminum foil, something like satin, something like well-tanned leather in its toughness, yet it was not precisely like any one of those materials. While I do not recall this with certainty, I think the fabric measured about four by eight or ten inches.... Bill passed it around and we all felt of it. I did a lot of sewing, so the feel of it made a great impression on me. It felt like no fabric I have ever touched before or since. It was very silky or satiny, with the same texture on both sides. Yet when I crumpled it in my hands, the feel was like that you notice when you crumple a leather glove in your hand. When it was released, it sprang back into its original shape, quickly flattening out with no wrinkles. I did this several times, as did the others."

The others told similar stories of the material. Loretta Procter said they tried to burn a small piece, about the size of a pencil, and failed. Jesse Marcel, Sr., said they hit a larger, metallic piece with a sledgehammer without doing any damage or marking the metal.

This body of firsthand testimony suggests that the debris found near Roswell was something extraordinary. The elements—foil that would return to its original shape without sign of a wrinkle or crease, extraordinarily tough metal that was as light as balsa but so strong that it wouldn't cut or break like ordinary metals, and something that sounded suspiciously like fiber optics at a time when no such thing existed on Earth—suggest the extraterrestrial.

A Question of Credibility

Redfern's theory hinges on the integrity of his anonymous, but alleged firsthand witnesses. Once, five or six years ago, there were a number of stories told by such witnesses about themselves, about what they had seen, and about alien bodies. Frank Kaufmann talked in detail about these things, as did Gerald Anderson, Jim Ragsdale, and Glenn Dennis. Kaufmann offered copies of official documents to prove who he was. He had a letter that, if authenticated, proved Roswell had been a spaceship crash.

Redfern, in an interview conducted for *UFO Review* (found at *www.uforeview.net*) said that the witnesses he refused to name had proven who they were by documents in their possession. To Redfern, this is proof that they are who they claim to be and that their tales can be trusted.

Yet the same could be said of Kaufmann. His documents looked authentic, and they were, after a fashion. Only after the originals were found could we see the alterations he had made to the copies he had given us. He'd used whiteout and a copy machine to forge documents to support his claims. Unless the original is available for scrutiny, documents are of little value. As Frank Kaufmann said, "The Xerox is as loose as a goose." Indeed, it is simple to forge documents in the modern age.

Redfern uses some of the Kaufmann testimony to bolster his case, seemingly unaware that Kaufmann invented his role in Roswell. If Kaufmann made up everything and had no role in the Roswell case, then where does that leave Redfern? He used Kaufmann's description of the craft to bolster his flying wing theory. Since we know that Kaufmann was inventing his tale, his testimony does nothing to support Redfern's theory.

The ET Hypothesis

If Redfern is wrong, and this wasn't some horrendous and illegal experiment, what is the answer? It's the same as it has been for the last two decades. It was extraterrestrial.

Redfern has suggested that his answer makes sense because he can find no documentation to support it. He reasons, with some logic, that those conducting the experiments, knowing that they were illegal, destroyed the evidence when they finished. The files were shredded, the remains of the craft were dismantled and burned, and those with knowledge were cautioned never to mention it to anyone.

Redfern tells us that an extraterrestrial craft would not lend itself to such a cover-up. Because the biological samples (alien bodies), the craft, and its components were unique, they would be preserved so that information could be gathered from them as our technology advanced. Indeed, logic argues in favor of this scenario: destruction of everything related to the case if it was an illegal experiment and preservation if it was extraterrestrial.

But there are other aspects that take us in the direction of the extraterrestrial. First is the credible eyewitness testimony about the surprising and unusual characteristics of the various materials recovered on the field northwest of Roswell. Clearly, these were things that were beyond the technology of the times and, in fact, some of them are beyond our technology today.

Second is the testimony of the witnesses who were on the scene. Jesse Marcel, Sr., said that this was something that came to Earth from elsewhere. As an air intelligence officer, he was in a position to know all there was to know about Earth-based craft. He knew about balloons and experimental aircraft, and he was convinced that what he found was none of those things.

Third is the testimony of Maj. Edwin Easley, the provost marshal at the base. In a conversation held about a year before his death, I asked him if we were following the right path. He wanted to know what I meant by that, and I said that we thought it was extraterrestrial. "Let me put it this way," he said, "it's not the wrong path."

Convoluted, and maybe a little confusing, but he, as a participant in the recovery, was telling me that the object that crashed was extraterrestrial. He confirmed that to family and friends in the weeks before he died.

Patrick Saunders, who was on Blanchard's primary staff in July 1947, also confirmed the extraterrestrial nature of the crash. Although he was always reluctant to talk about his involvement in the retrieval operation with UFO investigators, he did buy copies of *UFO Crash at Roswell*. He sent them to friends and family who asked him questions about the crash. On the flyleaf he wrote, "This is the truth and I never told anybody anything."

Roswell was not some rogue experiment using deformed and mutated Japanese captives, but the crash of an alien spacecraft. Those who were there would have recognized everything as terrestrial if that's what it was. The only answer that takes all the evidence into account is that this was truly something from another world.

A Response from Nick Redfern

September 2005

Kevin Randle's review of my book, *Body Snatchers in the Desert: The Horrible Truth at the Heart of the Roswell Story*, makes a number of comments and observations.

Randle's statements regarding the work of the Horten brothers are noted, but are not entirely crucial to the story, primarily because all of the interviewees told me that the aircraft that crashed at Roswell was based upon Japanese designs that were Horten-inspired, or Horten-like. But they were not built by the Hortens.

As Randle notes, in the 1940s the Germans were working with flying-wing-type aircraft (as per the Hortens), and so was the United States (with

Northrop). But I specifically point out that even though there was some likely collusion between the work of the Nazis and that of the Japanese, the device that came down at Roswell—according to the people I interviewed for the book—was Japanese and not German.

Randle says that the book provides a "nice theory" for the allegations that there was more than one crash site for the Roswell vehicle. It does. And we could argue that the reason why the theory is so "nice" is because it is the literal truth.

Randle disputes the possibility that the Japanese would have worked on postwar Fugo balloons that might have resulted in the creation of a hybrid-style device that was a blend of huge balloon array and flying wing. However, there is evidence to firmly demonstrate that the Japanese were working on far more ambitious balloon-based projects than the wartime Fugos.

For example, U.S. newspapers of 1945 talk about the Japanese planning to build far larger balloons that would have had a fully-pressurized gondola affixed to them piloted by "death-defying Japanese" for a manned assault on the U.S. mainland by balloon, after a four-day, high-altitude flight to the U.S.

Though Randle disputes the data contained within the book, he admits to speaking with a former White Sands employee who informed him of a theory that may have explained the unusual debris, and that may have incorporated a flying-wing-style vehicle in the accident. Randle states that the complete lack of official documentation in favor of this theory renders it unlikely at best.

However, Randle supports the extraterrestrial theory, for which there is also a complete lack of official documentation. One might ask: why does this lack of documentation offer greater support for the ET scenario?

The issue of the debris found at the Foster ranch and examined by a number of people—including Maj. Jesse Marcel— is certainly intriguing, and is one of the key aspects of the story that keeps people looking into it.

Yes, we have a lot of testimony that the debris was of an unusual nature. But consider the following: the only pictures we have of Marcel are with what is obviously balloon debris. The rancher, Mack Brazel, had previously found two balloons flown by the military on the same property. Brazel's daughter, Betty, said that: "The debris looked like pieces of a large balloon which had burst." It was also in this period that polyethylene balloons—laminated with aluminum—began to be used.

Even the Air Force stated that the descriptions of the debris that, when wadded into a ball, would resume its original shape, "are consistent with the properties of polyethylene balloons laminated with aluminum."

The biggest problem with Roswell is that it occurred nearly 60 years ago, and practically everyone involved is now dead.

The people with whom Randle spoke, who made seemingly pro-ET comments, either made very cryptic statements and are now dead (Easley) or made a one-sentence statement in a book (Saunders). How do we know that both men were not fed the "it was alien" line to further bury the truth, if anyone—such as Randle—came asking? I am certain that Easley and Saunders were not lying. But in the hall of mirrors known as Roswell, they may have been lied to by their superiors about the nature of what crashed at Roswell.

As evidence of this, my book includes a whole chapter ("The Crashed UFOs That Never Were") that details several occasions upon which the U.S. military and intelligence community deliberately spread bogus crashed UFO tales for disinformation purposes.

A thought to close on: If such disinformation could (as I show in the book) be applied at Aztec, New Mexico; at Spitzbergen, Norway; and at Kingman, Arizona; then why not at Roswell, too?

What Really Happened?

The question of what happened in Roswell, New Mexico, July 1947, has baffled researchers for years. Robert J. Durant, having investigated the controversy for over a decade, answers the question in a powerful and captivating 97-minute discussion with parapsychologist, Joanne D.S. McMahon, Ph.D. The interview highlighted by photos and film clips is accompanied by a simulcast from the Higgins Center featuring June Marlowe and a live audience.

Robert J. Durant, former Navy pilot, spent 31 years flying international routes for a major airline before his recent retirement. Durant has studied UFO phenomena since the 1950s and is a well-known author in the field. In recent years he has specialized in what the calls the Holy Grail of Ufology—Roswell.

"The best Roswell film I've seen"—Steven Spielberg

Roswell? Yes!
DVD, 97 minutes
$12.95 + shipping & handling

See order form on last page of this book.

As seen on TV...

Bob White saw a UFO on a lonely road in Colorado. Many people throughout the years have claimed to have seen a UFO, but Bob White is the only person to recover a piece of a UFO, write a notarized, sworn statement about his UFO encounter, pass a polygraph examination on the truth of his statements, and have the recovered UFO object tested at five major laboratories. In short, **Bob White has the hard evidence that UFOs are real!**

Much of the book consists of Bob's personal story of what he saw that night, how he recovered his hard evidence, and his subsequent search for the truth about the object. Bob has run into obstacle after obstacle from government and university scientists who won't tell him the complete truth about his hard evidence.

A startling development occurred when Bob found out the United States government had in its possession some UFO debris very similar to the hard evidence he recovered from the UFO. Obtained through the Freedom of Information Act, Bob includes these previously classified documents from the Central Intelligence Corps right after World War II, which lists the debris as from a "Flying Saucer from Denmark."

In 2003, Bob's object affected the electronic wall safe at the Harrah's Resort and Casino in Laughlin, Nevada. Further tests on the object revealed that it emitted electromagnetic radiation at X-ray or gamma ray wavelengths and exposed dental x-ray films. A NASA scientist has expressed an interest in testing the Bob White object to determine once and for all if it is extraterrestrial.

6 x 9, softcover, 126 pgs., photos, $14.95
**Comes with free CD:
"The Object" sung by Bob White**

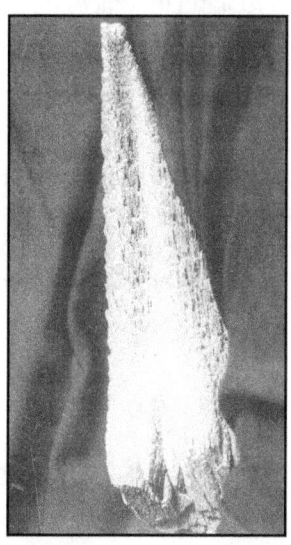

See order form on last page of this book.

No More Secrecy!

Author and UFO activist Larry W. Bryant has obtained much of this Carter UFO mail and presents the best of it, along with his astute commentary, in the new book, **UFO Politics at the White House**.

Some of the letters are cursory, others are cranky, and many are genuinely probing and informative. Bryant's book shows that when it comes to UFOs, the White House played—and continues to play—politics with one of the most important issues of our time.

UFO Politics at the White House features:

 • An in-depth foreword by respected UFO researcher Grant Cameron

 • A "story behind the story" essay from Bryant, detailing the book's genesis

 • An appendix surveying the UFO-related correspondence received by the presidential administration of Harry Truman

Jimmy Carter is the only U.S. president to admit to seeing a UFO. While running for office, he made a pledge to the American people to release all government information on UFOs if elected.

Carter became president, and despite a flood of mail from the public pleading for him to make good on his UFO promise, he failed to live up to his word.

UFO Politics at the White House

6 x 9 • softcover • 268 pgs.

$14.95 + shipping & handling

See order form on last page of this book.

Flying Saucers—
The Evidence Revealed

Focusing on possibly the greatest saga of all time, this book documents many fascinating events long forgotten by today's sound-bite generation. It is one of the very few books that approaches the subject of Unidentified Flying Objects (UFOs) from a historical perspective. The reports here are taken from the best sources available. The first chapters deal with the period from 1896 to 1946, a time of interesting legends and lore. In 1947, the first large wave of UFO sightings began with the famous sighting by pilot Kenneth Arnold.

By 1952 the most famous UFO wave unfolded. Incidents became so numerous in the U.S. that the Democratic National Convention in July had to fight for headline space with flying saucers—especially after they appeared over the White House! Fearing Cold War hysteria, the government discouraged future reports and investigations.

UFOs: A Century of Sightings does not stop there, however. Hall details the reports from the famous UFO flaps of 1954, 1957, the mid-60s, and 1973. Amazing encounters that have occurred since then are also discussed, including the most recent developments. This huge, illustrated, classic UFO book is chilling, mystifying, and amazing because it is a very real part of our history.

8-1/2 x 11 • softcover • 394 pgs. • illustrations

Special FATE sale price: **$24.95** (reg. $39.95)

See order form on last page of this book.

A barking dog announced the arrival of a stranger. The men in the house instinctively collected their guns—strangers were not very welcome in the backwoods of Kentucky after dark. When they stepped outside, they were approached by a being holding his arms over his head. He was dressed in a tight-fitting silver suit, and his peculiarly large eyes were six inches apart and shaped around the sides of a round, bald head with big floppy ears. The stranger stood only four feet tall and had a skinny, neckless body with arms hanging past its knees. Eagerly waddling toward their back door, the odd little creature was welcomed with a hail of fire from rifle and shotgun barrels. The interloper somersaulted to evade the bullets and ran for the woods as he men began to run in the opposite direction and into the house.

Then the fun began...

The Biggest UFO Coverup of All!

In *The Great UFO Hoax*, Kanon reveals a high-stakes game played by certain segments of government and industry to perpetrate a hoax on the American public. In an effort to cover up mind control and genetics experiments performed on ordinary citizens as well as new secret weapons, it became vital to convince people that UFOs were vehicles from other worlds.

Kanon draws on years of annotated research and accumulated evidence to demonstrate how this deception has been carried out. But most importantly, he explains why the perpetuation of this fraud has become so vitally important to a secret elite within our government.

Join Kanon and discover the truth behind the fraud.

6 x 9 • quality softcover • 224 pgs. • $14.95 + shipping & handling
See order form on last page of this book.

Help Make Our Extraterrestrial Friends Feel Warm and Welcome!

These durable hard plastic road signs look great on a wall or sitting on a desk. Or use them as coasters for that special intergalactic dinner party.

Choose **Alien Crossing** or **Flying Saucer Zone**

5 x 5 inch sign • $3.95 or 2/$5.95
12 x 12 inch sign $5.95 or 2/$9.95
See order form on last page of this book.

The Face of the Goddess?

Did extraterrestrial life visit both Mars and Earth in the far distant past? The answer to this question, according to newly discovered evidence presented in *Mars/Earth Enigma*, is an irrefutable yes!

What was the supernatural civilization responsible for leaving the same curious message on Earth and Mars—identical geometrically aligned pyramidal structures complete with humanoid faces? An enigmatic "skull and crossbones" best seen from the heavens?

In *Mars/Earth Enigma*, author DeAnna Emerson reveals, for the first time, the identity of this mystical extraterrestrial civilization, exploring detail by detail the tear in the eye of the face on Mars, and the strange markings on the face and head of the computer-enhanced features—an enigma so threatening to NASA that they promptly dismissed it as an "oddity of light and shadow," an image best forgotten.

Unraveling thread by thread the mysterious tapestry woven throughout history into one enigmatic picture, the author reveals, for the first time, the secret worshippers of the ageless and elusive "Mother of God," a mysterious ET-like being responsible for genetically creating mankind.

Mars/Earth Enigma explores the ancient Earth structures built by the descendants of the extraterrestrial Great Mother, sacred sites located in Egypt, Jerusalem, and most interestingly, Rennes-le-Château, the Grail area in France where pentagonal geometry associated with Mars and Earth is diagrammed in temples and other sacred sites built by the knights of the Crusades.

6" x 9" • softcover • 320 pgs. • illustrations and photos • $19.95

See order form on last page of this book

Keel Tells It Like It Is

John A. Keel has been entertaining, amazing, and infuriating readers since the 1940s. There's nobody quite like him; he's as much an anomaly as the puzzling creatures and events that he's been reporting on all these years.

This collection offers a lively sample of Keel's "Beyond the Known," the column he wrote for FATE for many years. Whether it was cryptozoology, World War II enigmas, fairies and wee folk, or things falling from the sky, Keel was always ready to hop into a car and track down weirdness where and when it was happening.

His wide range of interests—magic, comedy, religion, technology, philosophy, biology—give him a broad outlook and keep him curious. Keel has been a consultant for the Army and the Air Force; science editor for Funk & Wagnall's; and writer for television sitcoms. He has received honorary PhDs for his work in herpetology and archaeolo-

Conspiracy of the Ultraterrestrials
The Fortean Classic by **John Keel**

Is there a super race, not extraterrestrial but native to Earth, that predates Homo sapiens and has interacted with human history as both guardian and tormentor since prehistoric times? The existence of these beings would explain the strange phenomena and mysterious events that Keel explores to create a classic in the study of UFOs and Fortean phenomena.

Our Haunted Planet is based upon countless interviews, many in-depth personal investigations, and hundreds of books covering everything from alchemy to zoology. It asks many thought-provoking question about our strange world. In this collection of bizarre but true tales, John Keel, the renowned the respected author and researcher, brings into chilling focus strange truths about the Earth and its mysterious inhabitants.

6" x 9" • 224 pgs. • $14.95 plus shipping & handling
See order form on last page of this book

Here is evidence of:
- Advanced civilizations existing thousands of years before the cave man
- The strange Men in Black
- People who vanish and reappear within hours in another part of the world
- Mystic revelations throughout history that have led to nothing but illusion and ruin
- Abductions by aliens, elves, and gods
- Strange artifacts from the distant past that cannot exist—but do!
- Underground cults and conspiracies that are themselves tools of something even more hidden and even more dangerous

Now you can have <u>your own copy</u> of FATE
Vol. 1, No. 1, Spring 1948
featuring the famous Kenneth Arnold UFO sighting!

Authentic reprint of our very first issue complete with original ads and illustrations, 128 pages plus covers, just as it was in 1948

Now only **$14.95!**

• "Radio's Strangest Mystery" by Vincent H. Gaddis • "Mark Twain and Halley's Comet" by Harold M. Sherman • "Invisible Beings Walk the Earth" by R. J. Crescenzi • "Twenty Million Maniacs" by G. H. Irwin • "Science and the Soul" by R. P. Graham • More!

See order form on last page of this book.

Are the Watchers from Space?
Or Have They Always Been With Us?

THE ANCIENT EGYPTIANS called them the guardians, the *Neteru*. The most ancient civilizations of Mesopotamia called them the *Annunaki*. The ancient aborigines of Australia called them the *Wandjina*. They believed that it was these gods who created life on Earth. Early in the history of Judaism, multiple gods were recognized as the *Elohim*. Many times they are referred to as the sons of God. In the mystery texts of the Hebrews, the Books of Enoch (found among the Dead Sea Scrolls), they were called the Watchers. In the Gnostic texts of the first and second century, they were recognized as Archons. In the Bible they are referred to as angels, archangels, and as Watchers, but regardless of which culture we study, from the Native Americans to the indigenous peoples of the Amazon, Central America, or even Africa, the concept is the same. It has always been known that there are beings more advanced than the human race who have been involved with the Earth and its inhabitants for all time. **Today, we call these beings aliens or extraterrestrials and we call their craft unidentified flying objects: UFOs.**

Who are they? Where do they come from? Where do they go? Why are they here? How long has this been going on? How should we react to them? What should be our response to them as a society? Should we fear them, or should we revere and even worship them? No one has the answers.

6" x 9" • 252 pgs. • color illus. • $19.95

See order form on last page of this book.

Alien Crash Revisited
What Are the Facts?

In Roswell, New Mexico, on July 8, 1947, something strange happened. Something crashed. No one knew what it was, or, if they did, they weren't telling. Col. William Blanchard of the Roswell Army Air Field told Lt. Walter Haut, the Public Information Officer, to alert the local media. Haut produced a short press release that said that members of the 509th Bomb Group, there in Roswell, had recovered the wreckage of a flying saucer. Haut took the press release into town, delivered it to both newspapers and radio stations, and then went home for lunch.

Hours later Brig. Gen. Roger Ramey, photographed in front of some debris in his office at Eighth Air Force Headquarters, said that all the excitement was unwarranted. Nothing had been found but a weather balloon.

What was it? Why to this day does the Air Force refuse to admit what it really was? Why the lame explanations that explain nothing?

Today, we know more. We have overcome much of the confusion of the last decade, and we have some very strong evidence. We have solid eyewitness testimony from reliable sources who can prove they were in Roswell at the right time, they were in a position to know what was happening, and they have confirmed it. Now we need to finish the job, learning exactly what fell, and letting the world in on the greatest secret of the last thousand years.

6" x 9" • 182 pgs. • illus. • $12.95 + shipping & handling

See order form on last page of this book.

To order additional copies of this book,
please send full amount plus $5.00 for
postage and handling for the first book and
$1.00 for each additional book.

Send orders to:

Galde Press, Inc.
PO Box 460
Lakeville, Minnesota 55044-0460

Credit card orders call 1–800–777–3454
Phone (952) 891–5991 • Fax (952) 891–6091
Visit our website at http://www.galdepress.com

Write for our free catalog.

***To order books or items advertised here,
see order form on reverse of this page.***

Galde Press Order Form

PO Box 460, Lakeville MN 55044 • fax 952-891-6091
credit card orders call 1-800-728-2730

Name _____

Address _____

City _____ State _____ Zip _____

Daytime Telephone (_____) _____

Book Title/Merchandise	Qty.	Price	Total

Shipping & Handling					
No. of Items:	**1-3**	**4-6**	**7-10**	**Item Subtotal**	
U.S.	$ 5	$ 8	$10	**Minnesota Residents** add 6.5% Sales Tax	
Canada	$10	$15	$20	**Shipping & Handling**	
Int'l Surface	$15	$30	$45		
Int'l Airmail	$25	$40	$55	**Total Remittance**	

Shipping & handling fees subject to change without notice.

Method of payment:

☐ Check ☐ Money Order

☐ MasterCard ☐ VISA ☐ Discover ☐ American Express

Credit card _____

Expiration date _____

Signature _____

www.ingramcontent.com/pod-product-compliance
Lightning Source LLC
LaVergne TN
LVHW051827080426
835512LV00018B/2756